The Complete Guide to

Property Development

for the Small Investor

The Complete Guide to
Property
Development
for the Small Investor

3rd edition

CATHERINE DAWSON

KoganPage

LONDON PHILADELPHIA NEW DELHI

Publisher's note
Every possible effort has been made to ensure that the information contained in this book is accurate at the time of going to press, and the publishers and author cannot accept responsibility for any errors or omissions, however caused. No responsibility for loss or damage occasioned to any person acting, or refraining from action, as a result of the material in this publication can be accepted by the editor, the publisher or the author.

First published in Great Britain in 2006 by Kogan Page Limited
Reprinted in 2006
Second edition 2007
Third edition 2009
Reprinted 2010 (twice)

120 Pentonville Road
London N1 9JN
United Kingdom
www.koganpage.com

ISBN   978 0 7494 5451 7

British Library Cataloguing-in-Publication Data

A CIP record for this book is available from the British Library.

Typeset by Saxon Graphics Ltd, Derby
Printed and bound in India by Replika Press Pvt Ltd

Luxury for less

Pay less and you compromise on quality – well not anymore thanks to an entirely new concept in luxury vinyl woodplank flooring, which consistently delivers on price, quality, quick fitting, easy maintenance and remarkably good looks!

Senso, by vinyl flooring specialist Gerflor, provides anyone involved in new build or refurbishment with a real value for money flooring, which is comparable with the top brand luxury vinyl woodplanks, yet half the price and easier to fit.

It is however when installation times count that ready-to-install Senso really pays off. Super fast to fit, Senso comes with a pressure-sensitive, adhesive backing for easy, low cost installation without the need for tools – except a sharp cutting knife – separate adhesive, an insulating subfloor or a specialist fitter.

As strong as one of commercial quality and formulated to remain firm, the special, pre-applied adhesive automatically forms a perfectly sealed, waterproof join as it cures. The adhesive, which has undergone vigorous delamination testing, will not break down or become ineffective over time. However, should the need arise, the adhesive can be re-activated for easy replacement.

Senso captures the beauty of real wood in five distinctive ranges, each with a style of its own, and including an extra slip resistant option, two widths and many inspirational colours. It is coated with a clear, protective varnish making it especially resilient – it's even heel-proof – hygienic, easy to clean and without needing waxing or polishing.

Warm, comfortable and exceptionally quiet underfoot, Senso is suitable for every room including bathrooms, and an excellent alternative to real wood and laminate, which typically carry impact sound, especially in flats and apartment installations, where noise must be minimised.

For those preferring the look of tiles, Caractère, a luxury, ready-to-install vinyl tile range, has the same performance and installation benefits as the Senso collection. Caractère also accommodates the trend for larger tiles with a 40.6 cm x 40.6 cm tile and a new 45.7 cm x 30.5 cm tile.

Senso planks and Caractère tiles have a 10 year product guarantee. For further information visit www.sensobygerflor.com or telephone Gerflor on 01926 401500.

Senso

Floors to match your imagination

Safe as....

Choosing a new conservatory or replacement windows but don't know who to trust?

Every GGF member must work within our Code of Good Practice. Everyone that installs conservatories, windows and doors is also registered with FENSA to simplify working within the new Building Regulations. We offer a scheme to secure your deposit and even an arbitration and conciliation service if a problem can't be solved by other means.

So why not visit our home –www.ggf.org.uk– to find out why looking for the GGF logo helps you to rest easy in your home.

It can even help you to choose your installer with complete lists of members of our two specialist groups, the Conservatory Association and the Window and Door Group.

TRUST MARK
Government Endorsed Standards
Registered through:
Glass and Glazing Federation

Conservatory Association

GGF
Glass and Glazing Federation

Glass and Glazing Federation 44-48 Borough High Street, London SE1 1XB. **Tel:** 0870 042 4255 **Fax:** 0870 042 4266
e-mail: info@ggf.org.uk **website:** www.ggf.org.uk

Give your home kerbside appeal

Windows and Doors – what you need to know

Windows are the first thing people see when they visit your house, so it's no surprise to learn that badly fitted windows can affect the value of your home. Your best bet is to choose a member of the Glass and Glazing Federation (GGF).

Especially as all replacement glazing now comes under Building Regulations Control.

This means that if you want to replace your windows, those new windows will have to be energy efficient. The reason for this is the Government's drive to ensure we, like the rest of the world, pollute the atmosphere as little as possible.

If in the future you then decide to sell your property, the purchaser's solicitors, when undertaking the necessary search, will ask for evidence that any replacement windows installed after April 2002 comply with the new Regulations.

You can prove that your windows comply in two ways:-
1. a certificate showing that the work has been done by an installer who is registered under the FENSA Registration Scheme
   or
2. a certificate from the local authority saying that the installation has approval under the Building Regulations

If you want to ensure that you comply with these Regulations and that the company undertaking the work will do a good job, you should make sure that you use a Glass and Glazing Federation (GGF) member who is FENSA Registered.

Conservatories – let the light in!

Sunshine is a vital element in our lives. This is reflected in the popularity of holidays abroad in countries where temperatures are in the 90s and the sun is guaranteed. It is also apparent when people buy a new home. Recent surveys have indicated that home owners say the more light there is in their homes, the happier they feel.

The British craving for light is also indicated by the popularity of conservatories. During the Victorian and Edwardian periods, the conservatory was most often used as a winter garden, allowing plants to flourish all year round. These days, it tends to be used as extra living space, making the design specifications ever more important.

The majority of all conservatories built today are double glazed and allow the household to make year round use of their additional space and to appreciate the aesthetics and benefits provided by its glass walls.

As The Conservatory Association – a specialist division of the Glass and Glazing Federation – points out, conservatories can come in all shapes and sizes in both modern and traditional styles, but the one thing that unites them is glass. Glass enables us to sit in a conservatory even on a cold and blustery day, and bask in the sun.

What design?
Among the most popular designs are:

The Victorian
Characterised by a ridge with ornate cresting and multi faceted bay end – usually either 3 or 5 facets.

The Edwardian
Typically this has a square end which makes good use of space, and a pitched roof.

Lean-to
Great for both big and small awkward spaces like corners.

When you choose a GGF Member, you can be assured that they:

1. Will comply with the new Building Regulations (relating to windows) and ensure you get the appropriate certificate via the Fenestration Self Assessment Scheme (FENSA).

2. Will have been in business for at least three years.

3. Have all been vetted to ensure they provide a quality service, the vetting procedure includes taking up references, looking at their accounts and site visits.

4. Work to the Federation's Code of Good Practice and technical guidelines.

In addition the GGF will provide you with:

1. A free conciliation service – should you and a Member company not see eye to eye over work carried out.
2. Protection for your deposit – the GGF Deposit Indemnity Scheme is backed by Norwich Union and safeguards deposits up to £3,000 or 25% of the contract price, whichever is lower.
3. A Customer Charter.

TRUST MARK
Government Endorsed Standards
Registered through:
Glass and Glazing Federation

Contact us on: 0870 042 4255 for a list of members in your area or see www.ggf.org.uk

Contents

Stage Five: Perspiration

Stage Six: Presentation

Stage Seven: Preservation

Introduction

When this book was first written in 2006, investing in property was a lucrative and popular activity for many fledgling property developers and landlords. There was the opportunity to make large profits with careful investment and the buy-to-let and property development markets boomed as a result. However, over the last few months the property market has begun to suffer, with house prices in the first part of 2008 experiencing the largest single drop since the property market crash of 1992.

This has led some people to question whether investing in property is a wise decision to make. Others who have already invested in property are beginning to get nervous and are pulling out, selling their properties and investing their money elsewhere.

As a potential property developer you may also feel that the time is not right to continue with your plans. However, this is not necessarily the case. Professional property developers view the present market conditions as an opportunity to expand their portfolio. This is because there are many more bargains available, such as:

- properties that have been repossessed by the lender;

- properties that need to be sold quickly because the owner has fallen into arrears and needs to sell before their lender applies for a possession order;

- properties that have been sold quickly and cheaply by part-time investors who have got nervous about the credit crunch and falling house prices;

- failed buy-to-let properties, where a landlord has been unable to obtain the necessary rental income to make the investment viable.

All these properties have the potential to be offered for sale at below market value and provide the opportunity for investors to obtain a good deal.

Another important point to note is that many professional developers view their investment as a long-term strategy, especially if they are intending to let their property to tenants. They understand that the property market will always experience fluctuations, but if they buy wisely (the right property, in the right location, for the right price at the right time) they will almost certainly make a good profit on their investment over the long term. More information about knowing how to invest successfully in property during times of market uncertainty is provided in Chapter 1.

If you have decided that property development is still possible given the current economic climate, you can go on to decide what type of development is most appropriate for your circumstances. This book is aimed at investors who are interested in refurbishing, renovating, converting, building and letting property. It is divided into seven stages that guide you through the development process.

Stage One is the preparation stage, and includes decisions about the type of property development you wish to undertake, preparing yourself and your family, sorting out your finances, and making decisions about the type of business you wish to establish. Although mortgage companies are withdrawing their best mortgage rates and demand for mortgages has fallen to its lowest level since Labour came into power in 1997, there are still competitive deals available for property investors, and these are discussed in this part of the book.

Stage Two provides information about conducting background research, finding out about national and local housing prices and the performance of the property market, recognizing the potential for development and analysing the competition. This type of background research is of particular importance during times of market uncertainty. Therefore, this section of the book offers advice about avoiding the types of properties on which you could lose money, especially when property prices are falling. It also offers advice on finding bargain properties such as repossessions and failed buy-to-let investments properties.

Once you have conducted thorough research, Stage Three goes on to offer advice about procuring a property from viewing to purchase, whether this is done privately, through an estate agent or through auction. A viewing checklist is provided, along with advice about researching the neighbourhood and making sure that it is suitable for your intended market.

Stage Four offers in-depth advice about the legal aspects of property development. It includes information about planning permission, when it is required and how to make your application. Building regulations are also discussed, along with information about the Party Wall Act and avoiding boundary disputes.

In Stage Five the technical and practical issues of property development are discussed. This includes advice about developing and managing your budget; managing your project, either yourself or by appointing a project manager; working with builders and subcontractors; undertaking the building work yourself and sourcing materials. This stage includes important advice about health and safety.

Once your renovation, refurbishment and/or conversion project is complete, you need to think about presenting your property for sale or to let. Stage Six offers advice on how to do this, from deciding upon and understanding your market, to decorating and furnishing the property in the most appropriate way. Tips are offered on effectively and efficiently selling or letting your property.

The final stage considers preservation – looking after your property when it is let to tenants and knowing what to do if relationships break down or problems arise. This includes advice on taking tenants to court for rent arrears or eviction.

Property development has become increasingly popular over the last decade – there is potential for large profits to be made, but there is also potential for huge mistakes and financial loss, especially in times of market uncertainty. This book offers practical and technical advice on becoming a successful property developer and helps you to avoid common pitfalls. All the information you require is presented in one source, saving you considerable time and effort in your background research. Contact details of important organizations are presented for you to obtain specific advice relevant to your circumstances.

I hope you enjoy reading this book and find it useful and interesting. I wish you every success in your project.

Stage One
Preparation

1 Knowing how to invest successfully

Many potential investors are asking whether, given current market conditions, it is the right time to invest in property development. This is because property prices are falling in many parts of the United Kingdom and people are beginning to worry about the 'credit crunch' and the effect this will have on their family finances.

To be able to answer this question it is important to understand the relationship between the UK economy and the housing market, consider short- and long-term trends and undertake a full assessment of market conditions. It is also important to consider possible benefits for investors of the current market position, especially in terms of the availability of bargain properties such as repossessions and failed buy-to-let investment properties. Once you have considered these issues you can then ask whether it is prudent to invest in property development at this time. These issues are discussed in this chapter.

The economy and housing market

If you are thinking about investing in property development you need to have a thorough understanding of current and future economic and market conditions, and understand how they relate to the housing market. As we have seen in the United States, when the economy expands, lenders tend to extend too much credit and consumers are happy to accept this credit, usually because they have confidence in the housing market. This results in many people taking out larger mortgages than they can realistically afford, and leads to much greater borrowing on credit cards and hire purchase agreements. However, when economic conditions worsen, excessive borrowing means that people are unable to meet their payments, confidence in the housing market slumps, property prices begin to fall and homes are repossessed.

The International Monetary Fund (IMF) believes that the UK housing market will follow the US market, but on a two-year time lag. Experts fear that many homeowners in the United Kingdom who have overstretched their borrowing will suffer as a similar credit crunch begins and inflation rises. Indeed, recent figures indicate that the number of repossessions in the United Kingdom reached 27,100 in 2007, up from 22,400 in 2006 according to the Council of Mortgage Lenders (CML), and experts fear that this figure will rise to more than 45,000 in 2008. This has prompted the UK Government to begin talks with mortgage lenders to try to avert the crises and deal more favourably with homeowners who find themselves in arrears and facing repossession.

The role of the media

Some experts, however, think that the media in particular are over-emphasizing the financial problems being faced by the United Kingdom and that, in doing so, they are making a bad economic situation worse. Financial crises are always big news and the media has had some spectacular financial stories to report recently, including problems with rogue traders and bank collapses. Some people believe that this type of scaremongering could lead to people reducing their spending and saving money, which means that less money is spent and large amounts of money are removed from the economy. This can help to increase the likelihood of a recession and a property market crash.

One view is that buyers are being manipulated by stories in the media that do not reflect reality. This is because the media need to tell a story, but they also need to entertain, which often leads to a concentration of personal stories that do not reflect what is happening in reality. For example, I was recently approached by a TV company who wanted to interview me about the experiences of property developers who had lost their properties through repossession, or lost out financially through poor development strategies. I said that I didn't know of anyone that fitted this description. Our property company is doing very well and so are all the others that we are aware of. They were disappointed and said that this information would hardly make a good story. I pointed out that this reflected reality as I saw it. However, when the programme was screened it seemed to suggest that *all* property developers throughout the United Kingdom were suffering financially and that they were losing their properties through repossession. Two personal stories were reported to back up this assertion. Yet this does not reflect my reality – our company has been running successfully since 1996, and many of our competitors are also doing very well.

However, despite stories in the media not always reflecting reality, the media do have considerable influence on the public. Indeed, the Royal Institution of Chartered Surveyors (RICS) found in a recent survey that 23 out of 200 surveyors cited media gloom as having an impact on confidence in their local property market. If people are new to a particular market, such as property development, it is understandable that they will take note of the media when making investment decisions. However, you should balance this information with your own research. The economy in the United Kingdom is suffering, and there is potential for a property market crash, but this does not mean that property development is not still a viable investment opportunity, as long as careful decisions are made backed up by thorough personal research. Advice about how to do this is offered throughout this book.

Monitoring inflation

If you are thinking about investing in property development, it is important to monitor inflation and interest rates carefully to make the most of your investment. At this present time, the UK inflation rate is well above the Bank of England's 2 per cent target and above average for the European Union as a whole. Inflation determines the real return on any investment that you make and can have a major impact on the value of your investment in the future. This is of particular importance when viewing property investment as a long-term strategy. Therefore, you need to make sure that if you decide to invest in property development, your plans are not at the mercy of inflation and any future rises that may occur. In the United Kingdom the Consumer Prices Index (CPI) measures changes in the prices of selected household goods and uses this to determine the rate of inflation. For more information about the CPI and for up-to-date figures, visit www.statistics.gov.uk.

When economic growth is strong more money chases fewer goods and services, which pushes up prices and leads to higher inflation, which is what we have seen over the past few years in the United Kingdom. When this occurs, interest rates are used to keep growth broadly in line with its long-run trend of around 2.5 per cent each year. This is one of the reasons why interest rates rose in 2006 and 2007. Higher interest rates tend to discourage borrowing and encourage saving, which should slow the economy. Lower rates encourage borrowing and should have the opposite effect. This is one reason why we have seen the recent cuts in interest rates. Movements in interest rates affect the overall level of demand in the economy and so can have a powerful influence on the inflation rate.

Although higher inflation rates tend to be good for borrowers and bad for investors, you need to consider this link between inflation and interest rates when making your investment. If you intend to take out a mortgage on a property, the real value of your mortgage could be reduced considerably in times of high inflation, so this could work in your favour, but only if interest rates are favourable. Therefore, if you have cash to invest it may not be prudent to invest all of it in property by buying outright when inflation is high. Instead, you could decide to borrow on the property, or you could look to other types of investment. When doing this you need to consider the trends and prospects of other types of investment. Other assets, such as shares, can produce better returns than the property market, but this type of investment is much more volatile. In general, bonds and high-interest savings accounts will not provide as good a return as property has done over the last 35 years, but, in general, they are much safer options. If you are interested in other types of investment, you should seek the advice of an independent financial advisor. Information about doing so is provided in Chapter 4.

Understanding short- and long-term trends

To gain a better understanding of the trends and prospects of the housing market it is useful to look at how the market has performed in the past. Two useful house price surveys are produced by the Halifax and the Nationwide Building Society. The Halifax House Price Index was first produced in 1983. It shows that since then house prices have increased by 8 per cent a year, while inflation has increased by 4.5 per cent a year. The Nationwide house price survey began in 1973 and in that time house prices have increased by an average of 9 per cent a year. This compares to an average rate of inflation of 7 per cent a year over the same period.

These figures show that house prices have beaten inflation over the last 25–35 years, and that therefore buying property has represented a good long-term investment. Where investors can lose out is when they view their investment as a short-term strategy during times of market uncertainly. For example, in the five years from 1990 to 1995 house prices fell by around 10 per cent. Short-term investors who spent large amounts of money on properties and then tried to sell them lost out considerably during this time because prices were falling so quickly. However, in the 13 years since 1995 house prices have more than trebled in many parts of the United Kingdom. This means that, during this period, short-term property development strategies did prove to be very lucrative. Even people who bought properties that they sold on without doing any work were able to make a profit as prices were rising so quickly.

Currently we are experiencing another drop in the market. Therefore, there will be less opportunity for short-term developers to make a profit, whereas long-term developers can buy properties cheaply and keep hold of them until prices begin to rise again. If you are only interested in short-term development you *must* be very careful in your property choices if you are not to lose money on your investment. Advice offered throughout this book will help you to avoid investment mistakes.

Assessing market conditions

Opinion is divided about whether we will experience a property market crash. Experts have predicted that house prices will fall over the next two years anywhere between 5 and 40 per cent. As we have seen above, short- and long-term fluctuations in the housing market have always occurred and it is inevitable that an adjustment to the housing market will take place after the boom of the last decade. House prices have more than trebled in certain parts of the United Kingdom over that time and it is impossible to sustain this type of growth.

In March 2008 the Halifax reported that house prices fell by 2.5 per cent, which is the biggest single drop since the property market crashed in 1992. However, these figures do not reflect the whole story, as this kind of drop is not occurring in all parts of the United Kingdom. Indeed, house prices are still rising in some areas, such as parts of London, the East Midlands and parts of the South West.

However, as a potential investor you must be aware of the types of property that are rapidly losing their value and the areas that are dropping at a higher rate than others. For example, over the past decade buy-to-let investment has become very popular for part-time, amateur investors. Unfortunately, many of these people felt that it would be an easy way to make a large profit without putting in the required amount of work, again fuelled by over-the-top success stories reported in the media. This has led to investors making inappropriate decisions about when, where and what to buy, and many have paid too high a price for a property that is difficult to let.

Many of these investors are now getting the jitters, again due to media reports about a property crash. They, along with other buy-to-let investors, are trying to sell their properties. This has led to a number of similar properties appearing on the market at the same time, which has pushed prices down further and made the properties harder to sell. Although this is unfortunate for the people trying to sell, it creates more opportunities for potential buyers who can negotiate considerable price reductions. However, you must understand why the venture has failed in the past and make sure that you don't make similar mistakes. This involves undertaking a careful assessment of the current and future rental market in the area. Advice on how to do this is offered in Chapter 8.

Should I invest in property at this time?

With all the current and potential financial problems we are experiencing in the United Kingdom such as rising inflation, the increasing costs of mortgages and credit, and the rising cost of food and fuel, you are bound to be asking whether the present time is really the time to invest in property development.

Investing in property development can no longer be viewed as an easy way to make a quick profit, especially given current market conditions. However, it can be a lucrative and fulfilling venture if you are prepared to put in the required work and conduct all the necessary research. The property market is facing uncertainly over the next few years, but wise investors and full-time professionals who are in for the long haul know that property investment is safe and secure if they treat it with the respect it deserves. As long as you are careful, do your research and make wise decisions, then the time can still be right to invest in property development. Indeed, recent movements in the market, fuelled in part by the media scare stories mentioned above, has meant that there are more bargains available, if you know where to look and know how to compete with other property developers. At the moment it is a buyer's market and there are plenty of bargains available.

You need to undertake a careful assessment of your present and future finances when you think about investing in property development. It is important to consider these in terms of the amount you can afford to borrow, the interest rates you will have to pay and how these may rise or fall in the future. As the housing market begins to slow down, how will this affect your financial investment, over both the short and the long term? You must make sure that you do not put your family and your home at risk through unwise investment choices. Information and advice about doing this is offered in Chapter 4.

Also, as we have seen above, short- and long-term trends need to be taken into account when you consider your investment strategy. Although short-term strategies may still work in areas where property prices are rising, they will not work in areas where prices are falling. You must bare this is mind when developing your investment strategy.

Summary

To invest successfully in property you must understand the relationship between the UK economy and the housing market, consider short- and long-term trends and undertake a full assessment of market conditions. While present market conditions may not be so favourable for property developers who wish to renovate and refurbish to sell on, there is still plenty of potential for developers who see their investment as a long-term strategy. At this present time it is a buyer's market, which means that are a number of bargains available. However, you must make sure that you conduct thorough background research before making your investment. This is of particular importance during times of market uncertainty.

If you are hoping to invest in property development, there are a number of different strategies that you can adopt, depending on your family circumstances and finances, your skills, the property market and the area in which you live. These issues are discussed in the following chapter.

Useful addresses

British Bankers' Association
Pinners Hall
105–108 Old Broad Street
London EC2N 1EX
Tel: (020) 7216 8800
e-mail: use contact form on website
www.bba.org.uk

The British Bankers' Association (BBA) represents the banking industry in the United Kingdom. It is involved with the development and production of the Banking Code, produces a series of personal finance fact sheets for the general public, offers advice on money laundering and produces a variety of useful statistics and publications on finance in the United Kingdom. On the website you can access a variety of useful reports and statistics about the performance of the UK economy and the reaction of the BBA to latest trends.

Useful websites

www.bankofengland.co.uk

This is the website of the Bank of England. On this site you can find information about the Bank of England Base Rate, the current rate of inflation, the inflation target and detailed reports about inflation and interest rates.

Further reading

Dawson, C (2008) *The Complete Guide to Buying Repossessed Property,* Lawpack: London.

Making decisions

'Property development' encompasses a variety of ways in which to invest in property, and you need to think about the type of development in which you are interested. Perhaps you are interested in purchasing an empty property and renovating it for a family home? Or maybe you are interested in buying a suitable property to convert into flats to let to tenants? Or do you have a burning desire to buy some land and build your own home?

This chapter introduces the different types of property development, from renovation and refurbishment to conversion and new build. It also addresses the issues of becoming a landlord and providing housing for vulnerable and disadvantaged groups. This will help you to start to think about the type of property development that interests you, is feasible for your personal and family circumstances and appropriate for the present market conditions.

Refurbishing a property

'Refurbishing' involves the process of making cosmetic changes to a property to enhance its appearance to potential buyers or tenants. It does not involve alterations to the structure or fabric of a building.

Over the last decade refurbishing property has been popular with both home owners and property investors. This popularity was fuelled by success stories where home owners had made considerable profit on quite simple refurbishment. Currently there are still some properties to be found that have refurbishment potential – people are living longer, and older people are less likely to refurbish their existing property to modern tastes, even though the property may be well cared for. Once you have bought the property there are good opportunities to make simple changes without spending too much money. However, you must make sure that you buy the right property in an area in which property prices are still rising if you wish to undertake this type of development. Also, you will need to monitor prices carefully and make sure that you are able to sell when you can still make a profit.

Refurbishment is often a good starting point for someone new to the property business. An advantage to this type of development is that there is less chance to fail on your investment, if you buy in an area where property prices are still rising. A disadvantage is that there will be less profit available. Also, there is potential to make a considerable loss if property prices should fall quickly in the area in which the property is located. However, it does give you and your family the opportunity to test your skills and motivation to find out whether you really do want to become a property developer.

People who refurbish properties often live in that property while they are making the changes. This means that you would only have one mortgage and you can get a feel for the type of changes that would suit the property. Having a 'lived in' feel also helps potential purchasers to visualise the house as their future home.

To refurbish a property successfully you have to buy materials cheaply and make changes that will impress your potential market. Advice on sourcing materials is offered in Chapter 19. You also need to make decisions about your potential market before you begin the refurbishment – how your property is positioned in your mind may be very different from how it is positioned in the minds of potential buyers and tenants. Thorough market research is essential if you are to make a success of your refurbishment. Advice on doing this is offered in the second part of this book.

Renovating a property

'Renovating' a property means to restore it to its original condition through cleaning, tidying, repairing and/or rebuilding. In some cases this may involve improving the building so that it is better than its original condition. Renovating may involve alterations to the structure and the fabric of the building.

Renovation has become more popular, partly due to a growing environmental and conservation lobby that raises objections about new development on greenfield sites. Also, tax incentives are aimed at encouraging people to think more seriously about empty or run-down properties or developing on brownfield land. In addition to this, some local authorities are making the planning process easier for people who are interested in renovating an empty or run-down property, or are thinking about making environmentally friendly changes to an older property.

One of the most common ways for property developers to begin in the property business is to buy a property cheaply, renovate it and sell it at a profit. If you are new to property development and you are unsure of your skills and motivation, choose a property that does not require major work, but instead needs some updating, such as a new kitchen and bathroom. Making simple changes such as these can add considerable value to a property. However, you will need to develop a coherent business plan and carry out detailed market research to be successful in your renovation project (see Chapters 5 and 6). This is of particular importance during times of market uncertainty.

Empty properties

Empty properties can provide a good bargain if you are willing and able to carry out the required work. Often they are located in well-established residential areas, and you can find cheap properties in areas of regeneration that increase considerably in value once renovated. Properties are empty for a variety of reasons. The owner may have died or moved into a residential home; the owner may be unable to find the money to renovate, but is unwilling to sell; the Capital Gains Tax implications are too high and a family cannot afford to sell; a landlord is keeping hold of the property until prices rise and it is worth selling.

Most local authorities have a register of empty properties, and you may be able to find out who the owner is from this register, although some local authorities may be unwilling to share this information. If this is the case you can make a request for the information under the Freedom of Information Act 2000. Alternatively, you can find out whether the property is registered with the Land Registry, which, for a small fee, will provide the owner's details. For a list of Land Registry offices, visit www.landregistry.gov.uk. If this fails, check with neighbours to find out whether they have contact details for the owner.

Some mortgage companies are unwilling to lend on empty properties. However, there are some, such as the Ecology Building Society, Buildstore, the Co-operative Bank and the Norwich and Peterborough Building Society, which do provide mortgages on empty property. Other mortgage companies may offer a loan, but will release only part of the loan initially, with the full amount released once the works are complete. Some local authorities offer grants for renovating empty properties, and there may be reductions on VAT on refurbishment costs (see Chapter 4).

Property conversion

The most common type of property conversion is converting a large property to flats or bedsits. This is a larger-scale development and will need careful research and financial planning. Although initial financial outlay may be much greater, the potential for larger profits is also greater. However, the potential for all kinds of development and financial problems increases with larger developments, so you will need to think very carefully about your skills and motivation before you decide to follow this route.

If you are thinking about converting a property, you also need to make decisions about whether you intend to sell the flats as individual units, or let them to tenants and manage the property, either by employing a property management company, or by doing it yourself. Again, when making these decisions you will need to take note of short- and long-term fluctuations in the market (see Chapter 1).

If you decide to let the flats or bedsits, you need to find out whether your property will be defined as a House in Multiple Occupation (HMO). If so, you should be aware that special rules and regulations apply to HMOs. You will need to make sure that your conversion meets required standards in terms of numbers, type and quality of shared bathrooms, toilets and cooking facilities, and in terms of health and safety.

Most HMOs must be licensed, and to become a licence holder you must be a 'fit and proper' person. If you have convictions for violence, sexual offences, drugs or fraud you may not be granted a licence. Also, if you have ever contravened any laws relating to landlord and tenants, or other housing issues, or you have ever been found guilty of any discriminatory practices, you may find it hard to obtain a licence.

A licence normally lasts for five years and can be revoked at any time if conditions are breached. Local authorities have been allowed to set fees at their own discretion, so contact them direct to find out how much a licence will cost. If you are thinking of following this route, you need to be committed to your development and make sure that you develop a comprehensive business plan (see Chapter 5). For more information on HMOs, contact the Department for Communities and Local Government (details below).

Although conversion projects are expensive and need careful planning, they too have become popular in recent years. This is partly due to government incentives and tax breaks that have made conversion projects financially viable (see Chapter 4). It is also due to the conservationist lobby that would rather see the redevelopment of existing buildings than the use of greenfield sites for development.

Undertaking a new-build project

Building a new house is perhaps the largest type of property development you might undertake, especially if you intend to manage the project yourself. There are several advantages to new build. You can build in a location of your choice, build to your personal specifications and achieve a great deal of satisfaction on completion of the project. There is also the opportunity to make large profits. The disadvantages are that suitable building land is becoming harder to find, you have to become very familiar with Building Regulations and the planning system, and will be constrained by rules and regulations, the project can be time-consuming and stressful, cash flow can be a problem, and the development can eat up a large amount of your existing budget.

New build should only be carried out by those who are fully committed to the project and who have the finance to back up their ideas. New build is becoming more popular, and it is now possible to obtain a new-build mortgage which provides some of the finance up front so that you don't have to sell your existing home or move into rented accommodation while you are building your property.

One reason for the popularity of new build is more demand for eco-friendly ways of living. New houses provide this opportunity as they can be built with energy efficiency in mind, with good insulation, energy-saving devices and lower running costs. Also there are some government incentives and tax savings available for new-build projects (see Chapter 4). For more information about buying, selling and investing in green property, see Further Reading.

Becoming a landlord

Becoming a landlord involves a wide range of issues, not least coming to terms with the complex rules and regulations set by the government. You will also need to think about your business plan and marketing strategy. This includes decisions about how you intend to present your property, to whom and for what price (see Chapter 5).

It is worth noting that, whatever cycle the housing market follows, there will always be a demand for rented accommodation. Over the last few years many people have been priced out of the housing market and have had to rent until house prices are lowered or they have enough savings. If the housing market crashes, there will be many unfortunate people who cannot keep up with their mortgage repayments and will need to take advantage of rented accommodation. There will always be people who do not want to buy a house, and there will always be people who can't afford to buy a house.

Housing for vulnerable and disadvantaged groups

Vulnerable and disadvantaged groups often find it difficult to obtain suitable accommodation. As a landlord you might want to consider offering property to the following types of people who struggle to find landlords willing to offer them accommodation:

- pensioners;
- refugees;
- people with disabilities;
- low-income groups;
- ex-offenders.

If you decide to take this route, seek appropriate advice, as some of the tenants may be more challenging and demanding, but your role as landlord can be much more rewarding. Useful addresses are provided at the end of this chapter.

Becoming a registered social landlord

If you are committed to providing accommodation for disadvantaged groups, you should think about becoming a registered social landlord. To do this you will need to be a registered charity or a company that does not trade for profit. You will also need to demonstrate your financial viability by producing a detailed business plan (see Chapters 4 and 5). The Housing Corporation provides information and advice for landlords considering this option (details below).

If you are considering taking this route, extra financial support may be available to you. For example, in Scotland a housing association grant is available to registered social landlords to acquire land or buildings and to build, convert or improve housing for rent or low-cost home ownership. For more information consult the Communities Scotland website: www.communitiesscotland.gov.uk.

Summary

If you are a potential property developer it is important to spend time thinking about the type of property development that interests you. The term 'property development' covers a wide area and some types of development will be more suitable than others.

You need to think about the type of property development in terms of your own goals and aspirations and those of any family members who may also be involved in the business. You also need to think about your skills, motivation and commitment, and those of other family members. These issues are discussed in the next chapter.

Useful addresses

Department for Communities and Local Government
Eland House
Bressenden Place
London SW1E 5DU
Tel: (020) 7944 4400
Fax: (020) 7944 4101
e-mail: use enquiry form on website
www.communities.gov.uk

The Department for Communities and Local Government (CLG) was created on 5 May 2006. You can obtain information about HMOs, the new home information pack and other useful housing information from its website.

The Housing Corporation
Maple House
149 Tottenham Court Road
London W1T 7BN
Tel: (0845) 230 7000
Fax: (020) 7393 2111
e-mail: use enquiry form on website
www.housingcorp.gov.uk

The Housing Corporation is the government agency that funds new affordable homes and regulates housing associations in England. Details about how to become a Registered Social Landlord can be obtained from its website.

HACT
50 Banner Street
London EC1Y 8ST
Tel: (020) 7247 7800
Fax: (020) 7247 2212
e-mail: hact@hact.org.uk
www.hact.org.uk

HACT is a registered charity and development agency that 'aims to develop and promote solutions for people on the margins of mainstream housing'. At present it has three main programmes: the refugee programme, the older people's programme and the supported living programme. Grants are available for housing projects related to these programmes. If you are interested in providing housing for any of these groups, staff will be able to offer advice.

Shelter
88 Old Street
London EC1V 9HU
Tel: (0808) 800 4444
Fax: (0844) 515 2030
e-mail: info@shelter.org.uk
www.shelter.org.uk

Shelter is a housing charity that campaigns to end problems with homelessness and bad housing. Each year it helps thousands of people fight for their rights, improve their circumstances and find and keep a home. The charity will offer advice and guidance to anyone thinking about providing accommodation for vulnerable groups. Useful information, advice and guidance are available on its website covering most aspects of renting, leasing and letting property. Shelter also produces a number of useful publications that can be ordered online.

The Empty Homes Agency
Downstream Building
1 London Bridge
London SE1 9BG
Tel: (020) 7022 1870
Fax: (020) 7681 3214
e-mail: info@emptyhomes.com
www.emptyhomes.com

The Empty Homes Agency is an independent campaigning charity that aims to highlight the waste of empty homes in England. It works with a number of organizations to provide solutions to the problem and bring empty property back into use. On the website you can obtain a statistical breakdown of empty property figures in England by local authority. Useful advice on all aspects of purchasing an empty property can be obtained from the website.

Useful websites

www.landregisteronline.gov.uk

Land Register Online provides easy access to details of more than 20 million registered properties in England and Wales. You can download copies of title plans and registers in PDF format for £3 each, payable online by credit card.

Further reading

Dawson, C (2008) *Green Property: Buying, Developing and Investing in Eco-friendly Property*, 2nd edn, Kogan Page, London

Preparing yourself and your family

Once you have thought about the type of property development in which you would like to get involved, you need to think about preparing yourself and your family for the new investment. This involves an analysis of your personal skills, knowledge, commitment and motivation, and the same analysis for any family members who are to be involved in the project.

This chapter offers advice about developing and analysing your skills of reflection, realistically assessing your skills, knowledge and experience and conducting a self-evaluation. It goes on to offer advice about ways of improving and developing your skills.

Developing your skills of reflection and analysis

If you are hoping to become a successful property developer, it is important to develop your skills of reflection and analysis. This is because these skills will help you to understand what you already know about the property market and enable you to use this information efficiently. It will also help you to sift through and analyse information that is provided from a variety of sources. Through careful analysis and reflection you will come to understand when information is reliable and accurate and when it may be sensationalist and less reliable. This is of particular importance when rumours abound about an imminent market crash and recession. Reflective thought involves the ability to acquire facts, understand ideas and arguments, analyse and evaluate information and produce conclusions. It includes the ability to question and solve problems by linking your previous ideas, knowledge and experiences with present ideas, knowledge and experiences. You will find the reflection process easier if you consider the following points:

■ Your ability to reflect increases as you create mental challenges for yourself.

■ Social interaction aids reflection, especially when this interaction is with people who have the same interests and business, such as landlords and property developers.

■ Reflection becomes easier the more you know about a topic. Thorough property research is vital.

■ Your ability to reflect is increased by surrounding yourself with others who are engaged in reflection about a similar topic. This is one reason why joining landlord associations and/or neighbourhood groups is so important.

■ Reflection is more effective if carried out in an appropriate environment free from distraction.

■ Constructive feedback, and the support of family and friends, helps your ability to reflect.

You have a great deal of housing experience on which to draw. Through reflecting on this experience and through acquiring further information to build on this experience, you will find that you begin to make the right decisions when choosing and buying property.

Assessing skills, knowledge and experience

When assessing skills, knowledge and experience you need to carry out the same assessment for everyone intending to be involved with the property business. Successful business requires commitment and motivation from all involved. Find out the strength of this commitment and determine whether goals and aspirations between family members are the same. Each person involved in the investment should consider the following questions:

■ What are your five main reasons for buying a property for investment?

■ What are your short-term property investment goals?

■ What are your long-term property investment goals?

■ In terms of investing in property, what are your personal strengths?

■ In terms of investing in property, what are your personal weaknesses?

■ What action do you intend to take to overcome your weaknesses?

■ If others are to be involved in the investment, what strengths can they bring to the investment?

■ If others are to be involved in the investment, what weaknesses do they have which could influence the success of the investment?

■ What action will they take to overcome their weaknesses?

■ Do you have the personal support of all members of your family? If not, how do you intend to overcome problems?

■ Do you have any worries and concerns about investing in property? If so, what are they and how do you intend to overcome them?

■ What type of property investment are you looking for?

■ What do you see as the significant trends and prospects in the market of your chosen investment?

■ What opportunities are available in your preferred method of investment?

■ What are the threats to, and problems with, your preferred method of investment?

■ Have you carried out adequate primary and secondary research into your chosen investment? If not, what do you intend to do to rectify this? (See Chapter 6.)

▌ Do you anticipate any financial problems, either now or in the future? If so, what action are you going to take to reduce problems? (See Chapter 4.)

▌ What time do you have available to spend on your property investment? Will this be adequate?

▌ What contingency plans do you have in place, should your investment fail?

▌ Are you putting your home and family at risk in any way, especially financially and emotionally?

▌ What are the personal and/or family advantages to investing in property?

▌ What are the personal and/or family disadvantages to investing in property?

▌ Have these been discussed with everyone who is to be involved in the decision to invest?

Once these questions have been answered on an individual basis, they should be discussed thoroughly so that you can check that you have compatible ideas, goals and aspirations for your business.

Developing skills

After having completed your self-assessment, you may find that you need to improve or update some of your skills. Further education colleges or adult education services will provide short, informal courses and longer courses leading to recognized qualifications in areas such as bricklaying, bookkeeping, plumbing, and decoration and design. Contact your local college and/or adult education service, or consult the following websites:

▌ **www.learndirect-advice.co.uk**   Through this site you can access the learndirect course database which contains details of thousands of different courses and learning opportunities in a wide variety of subjects. Or you can ring the help line for further advice (tel: 0800 100 900 in England, Northern Ireland

and Wales or 0808 100 9000 in Scotland). If you live in Scotland, visit www.learndirectscotland.com

■ **www.careerswales.com**   Careers Wales Online provides careers-related information and advice for all age groups, which includes information about thousands of courses in Wales. The website contains a section on learning choices which enables you to find a course close to your home in Wales.

■ **www.careers-scotland.org.uk**   Careers Scotland provides a starting point for anyone looking for careers and learning information. The website includes information about learning choices and financial help for students who wish to study in Scotland.

If you are hoping to become a landlord, the Residential Landlords Association and the National Landlords Association provide a variety of seminars, training events, conferences and forums that help you to improve and update your skills and knowledge (details below). The relevant professional body will also be able to offer advice about professional training – contact details are provided in the 'useful addresses' section at the end of this book.

Summary

To be successful in your property business you and anyone else involved in the business should be thoroughly committed to the project. Reflect on your existing knowledge and experience, making sure that you have realistically assessed your skills and knowledge and that you know how to develop appropriate skills if these are lacking. This assessment should include family members and partners who intend to become involved with your venture. During this reflection process you should learn to analyse information from a variety of sources, so that you can assess the validity and reliability of any new information you find.

Once you have conducted a careful assessment of your skills, motivation, experience and commitment, you need to think about your finances. Financial advice is offered in the next chapter.

Useful addresses

Educational Guidance Service for Adults
4th Floor, 40 Linenhall Street
Belfast BT2 8BA
Tel: (028) 9024 4274
Fax: (028) 9027 1507
email: use online form
www.egsa.org.uk
If you live in Northern Ireland contact the Educational Guidance Service for Adults (EGSA). This is an independent, voluntary organization that aims to put adults in touch with learning opportunities by providing a comprehensive advice and guidance service.

National Landlords Association
22–26 Albert Embankment
London SE1 7TJ
Tel: (020) 7840 8900
Fax: (0871) 247 7535
e-mail: info@landlords.org.uk
www.landlords.org.uk
The National Landlords Association (NLA) provides a range of benefits and services to members including a telephone advice line, regular journals, meetings, events and fact sheets. You will need to pay a membership fee if you decide to join – details of fee levels are available on the website.

Residential Landlords Association (RLA)
1 Roebuck Lane
Sale, Manchester M33 7SY
Tel: (0845) 666 5000
Fax: (0845) 665 1845
e-mail: info@rla.org.uk
www.rla.org.uk
The Residential Landlords Association arranges free telephone support, produces a members' magazine, arranges meetings and training and provides free tenancy agreements. There is a fee to pay if you decide to join. More details are available on their website.

4 Sorting out your finances

Most people who wish to invest in property will need to raise some extra financial support. Even if you are in the lucky position of having enough cash to purchase your property, it may not be prudent to do so. Unforeseen or unexpected expenses can arise at any time during the development, and you need to make sure that you have enough available cash to deal with the problems when they occur.

This chapter offers advice about assessing your personal finance, obtaining financial backing, speaking to professionals, obtaining a mortgage and understanding tax implications.

Assessing your financial circumstances

Think about your financial circumstances in relation to the present and to the future. A common mistake is to consider this issue only for the present. Although interest rates have been falling recently, they will rise again over the next few years. If this is the case, will you be able to meet your mortgage repayments in the future?

Members of the Bank of England's Monetary Policy Committee (MPC) have pointed out their concern that the consumer boom that was keeping the UK economy afloat was being driven by people cashing in on high house prices. If the housing market crashes, people will find themselves with huge debts that rapidly become unmanageable. This will drive down consumer spending and could plunge the economy into recession. The housing market is directly linked to the economy. It is important, therefore, to understand the market and current economic conditions before borrowing large amounts of money that you might struggle to pay back (see Chapter 1).

To avoid facing such problems you should not only carefully assess your personal finances, but also consider the views and arguments of market and economic experts. It is also important to look at market circumstances from a historical point of view. The house price boom has now vastly exceeded levels of the 1988/89 boom which ended in high interest rates, negative equity for many home owners and a recession.

If you are expecting to take out a mortgage, you should ask the following questions:

▮ Will taking out a mortgage on a development property influence my chances of getting a mortgage if I decide to move house at a later date?

▮ Can I afford to lose money or take a loss if the housing market slumps?

▮ Can I weather fluctuations in the market?

▮ Can I continue with my development project and make mortgage payments if I am prevented from working/earning due to illness?

▮ Will I be able to cover mortgage payments and insure the property if I have no money coming in from rent?

▮ Can I afford to have a deposit tied up in a property for an indefinite period?

Obtaining financial backing

There are several types of finance available, and you need to think about the type of finance that best suits your needs. These include:

▮ investment by an individual in the form of either capital or loans;

▮ institutional investment, either of capital or loans;

■ bank loans, overdrafts and credit cards;

■ grants, loans and other assistance from the government or local authority;

■ hire purchase or leasing;

■ loans against endowment and pension policies;

■ mortgages and second mortgages.

If you need financial backing, you have to convince a lender or an investor that you and your ideas are worth backing. You will need to sell yourself, the viability of your ideas, your stability and your reliability. To do this you need to have a firm belief in what you are doing, plan carefully and be prepared for meetings with potential backers.

In addition to drawing up a business plan (see Chapter 5) you should carry out the following:

■ Identify and prioritize your short-term and long-term goals.

■ Check your existing resources and think about how you would like these to improve in the future.

■ Seek appropriate, impartial advice from an expert (see below).

■ Shop around for the best deal and choose products/investors suitable for your needs. Don't accept the first offer of cash. Keep your options open.

■ Don't rush into decisions. Discuss options with family and/or business partners.

■ Review your financial situation on a regular basis.

When obtaining backing, a lender/investor will want to see your business plan, profit/loss plan and cash flow forecast. Depending on the amount you wish to borrow, you may be asked for a personal guarantee and a charge on the assets of your business and your personal assets. If you are providing this, you need to make sure that family members and/or business partners are aware of it and understand the implications.

Knowing about mortgages

The general rule used to be that people were able to borrow either three-and-a-half times their own salary, or three times the salary of the highest earner and one times the salary of the second earner. However, in a bid to secure custom during the housing boom of the last decade, some lenders were willing to provide much more than this amount. Also, they were willing to provide a loan of 100 per cent or 125 per cent of the value of the property when house prices were rising rapidly.

However, the credit crunch has led to most mortgage companies moving away from their higher-risk lending, with many withdrawing their 125 per cent loans and some now withdrawing their 100 per cent loans. Also, they are much less willing to loan money to people with 'adverse credit'. This is a term that is used in official financial documents to describe bad credit, that is, someone who is considered to be a high risk to lenders because they have experienced financial difficulties in the past, missed payments or had debt recovery proceedings started against them. The term 'sub-prime' has recently become popular to describe this type of borrower, especially when discussing the crises in the United States. If you fall into this category, unfortunately you will find it much harder to obtain a mortgage without having a very large deposit.

Also, given the current concern with global lending, many mortgage companies are withdrawing their best mortgage deals or are only willing to lend to existing customers or those that have at least a 20 per cent deposit. This is not to say, however, that there are not good deals still available. If you require a mortgage you should shop around for the best deal, using one of the mortgage comparison websites available on the internet, or by seeking the advice of an independent financial adviser who specialises in mortgages.

In most cases you will find that you will be able to obtain a better deal if you can pay a larger deposit, but you must make sure that you have enough money available for the development of your property. When finding a suitable mortgage, be aware of the large arrangement fees that tend to be attached to the most attractive rates. These fees are only worth paying if you are borrowing a large amount of money and can recoup the fee on the amount of interest you will save over the term of the mortgage.

You should note that mortgage deals are changing much more quickly than they used to, so to make the most of the best deals you must be able to move quickly on your house purchase and mortgage arrangements.

When choosing a mortgage, consider whether you want an interest-only mortgage (your repayments only cover the interest on your loan) or a repayment mortgage (you gradually pay off the amount you owe). You also need to think about the following types of interest rate deals:

- standard variable rate – your payments go up and down when your lender's mortgage rate changes, usually in line with the Bank of England base rate;

- tracker rates – this is a variable rate loan which tracks changes in the base rate, at an agreed rate for an agreed amount of time;

- fixed interest rate – your repayments are set at a certain level for a fixed period of time, and will usually revert back to the standard rate after the agreed period;

- discounted interest rate – payments are variable, but set at a rate less than the standard rate for a set period of time;

- capped rate – your repayments are variable and linked to the base rate but are 'capped' and will not go above a set level during the period of the deal;

- collared rate – this may be used in conjunction with a capped rate and/or tracker mortgage; payments are variable, but will never fall below a set level;

- standard variable rate with cash back – this is similar to a standard variable rate mortgage, but once you have taken out the loan you will receive a sum of cash, which could amount to 5 per cent of your loan.

Buy-to-let mortgages

These mortgages are designed to help private individuals invest in property to let without being penalized by extra charges or high interest rates. They are not the same as mortgages provided on a home in which you want to live. Instead, the mortgage lender will want to know the letting and income potential of the property, rather than your personal income. It will want to know that you are thoroughly aware of the market conditions in the area and that you have conducted comprehensive market research.

When you arrange a buy-to-let mortgage you will be subject to the same status checks as with any mortgage. In general, you will be able to arrange a loan for anywhere between 5 and 45 years and from 15 to 80 per cent of the purchase price. The mortgages are usually about 0.5 per cent higher than a normal standard variable rate mortgage and are available in long, short, fixed or capped options.

As with other types of mortgage there are still some good buy-to-let deals available, although you will need to shop around for the best deal. These will be more favourable if you are able to pay at least a 20 per cent deposit. However, you should note that some mortgage companies will not lend money for some city centre buy-to-let apartments as these are becoming increasingly difficult to let. Heed the advice of your mortgage company – if they are unwilling to lend on a property, find out why and consider moving onto something that represents a better investment.

Self-build mortgages

These mortgages are offered on property under construction. The loan is paid out in stages so that the loan to value rate does not rise too high at any point. This is a percentage figure of the loan amount in relation to the property value. It is possible to receive up to 95 per cent of the final value of the property, or 95 per cent of the total costs of the project, which includes purchase of the land or property.

Self-certification mortgages

Most lenders will want proof of your income before they will offer a mortgage. However, if you are self-employed or find it difficult to provide proof of your income, you can complete your own assessment of income. If you decide to follow this route, you must make sure that you do not overstate your income, as you could struggle to pay back your loan, and it is a criminal offence to lie about the level of your income.

Ethical mortgages

Some banks and building societies have set up mortgages that support environmental projects. For example, the Co-operative Bank and the Norwich and Peterborough Building Society both offer mortgage products linked to reforestation schemes. Also, a number of ethical fund providers offer house purchase endowment products through ethical funds. More information about ethical investors can be obtained from the Ethical Investment Research Service (details below).

If you are interested in obtaining a mortgage for properties that give an 'ecological payback' you should contact the Ecology Building Society (details below). This includes energy-efficient housing, ecological renovation, derelict and dilapidated properties and small-scale ecological enterprises. For more information about green property issues, see 'Further reading' in Chapter 2.

Incentives

Some mortgage lenders will offer special deals or incentives to encourage customers to borrow. This could be a free valuation, payment of legal fees or an offer of cash back. However, before you accept this type of incentive you need to think about the future. If you will ever be in the position to pay off your mortgage early, or if you decide to change lender, you will have to pay back the incentive. Also, the cost of the incentive will usually be added to the price of the mortgage in some form, so you need to work out whether the mortgage with incentive provides the best deal in the long run.

Comparing mortgages

The FSA website provides a useful comparative table for mortgages, enabling you to search for, and compare, the types of mortgage that might suit your needs. Although the products mentioned are not recommendations, it provides a useful resource to help you to begin your research into mortgages. You can also find useful information about the types of mortgage on offer, and advice about avoiding pitfalls when choosing a mortgage. A handy mortgage calculator helps you to work out how interest rate rises will affect your mortgage payments (details below).

Seeking advice from professionals

Before you pay out large sums of money for your property investment, you should seek impartial advice from experts. Not only does it save you many hours of research time, but somebody who knows about mortgages, insurance and/or taxation issues could save you thousands of pounds by identifying a financial product appropriate to your needs and circumstances. Professional advice is of particular importance during times of market uncertainty.

Obtaining mortgage advice

Only firms and their agents authorized by the FSA are allowed to give advice about mortgages, and they must follow certain rules when offering advice. First they must give you a document that details the service they can provide. This should include details about whose mortgages they offer and whether there is either an upfront fee payable or commission. Second they must give you a key facts document that summarizes the important features of their mortgage. Once you have received advice you will then receive a personalized illustration of key facts about the mortgage.

Employing an accountant

If you decide to employ an accountant you should check that he or she has professional indemnity insurance, as this will protect you for any loss suffered through the fault of the accountant. If you choose a chartered accountant he or she will be backed by a rigorous disciplinary regime which means that you can complain to the Institute of Chartered Accountants in England and Wales if you are not satisfied (details below).

When you first employ an accountant he or she should send you an engagement letter which includes information about the terms of trade, the fees and how to complain if you are not satisfied with the service. Your accountant should respond promptly to telephone and written enquiries, and should ensure that all work is carried out to a reasonable standard and within all expected time frames.

Understanding tax implications

If you are entering into the trade of property development, and you have not set up a company, you will be taxed on an income tax basis on that trade, which, in the absence of any other agreement, would be in proportion to the amount of profit you make each year. If you let your property you will be liable to pay tax on your net income from rents. However, you can deduct your day-to-day running expenses from this income. You will need to keep all records of income and expenditure and complete a self-assessment tax return each year.

One of the advantages of setting up a company is that the corporation taxes are approximately half as high as income tax and Capital Gains Tax rates (see Chapter 5). However, withdrawing money from the company will attract a tax liability.

As a property developer, there are other taxes, allowances and exemptions that may be of interest to you. Some of these are listed below. More information about all these schemes can be obtained from HM Revenue & Customs (www.hmrc.gov.uk).

Stamp Duty Land Tax

Stamp Duty Land Tax (SDLT) was introduced in December 2003 and replaces stamp duty. The duty must be paid on all land transactions over a certain amount – for current rates see Chapter 15.

However, the government has introduced an exemption on SDTL for residential property transactions in the most disadvantaged parts of the United Kingdom. This scheme has been introduced to help promote urban regeneration and encourage families to relocate to these areas. You can use the Postcode Search Tool on the HM Revenue and Customs website to find out which areas qualify for relief.

Capital Gains Tax

Capital Gains Tax (CGT) is payable by the individual taxpayer on gains arising from the sale of securities or other chargeable assets, which include property. In general you will not have to pay CGT on the sale of your home if you used it primarily as your home and you have not used it for any other purpose during the time that you have owned the property. However, CGT is payable on a property that is not your main home, such as a development or tenanted property, although you may be entitled to claim relief against some or part of the gain. This could include deductions of some of the costs of buying, selling and improving the property.

CGT rules can be complex and you should seek professional advice when working out how much CGT you have to pay.

Flat conversion allowances

This scheme was introduced in the Finance Act 2001. If you are interested in renovating or converting vacant space above shops or other commercial buildings, and you intend to let the flats, this scheme enables you to claim up-front tax relief on your capital spending.

To qualify for the scheme the property must have been built before 1980, it must not be more than four storeys high and the storeys above ground floor level should have been unoccupied or only used as storage for at least a year prior to the proposed conversion. Also, the conversion must take place within the existing boundaries of the building, and each new flat must be self-contained with separate access, to be let on a short-term basis.

Reduced VAT for residential conversions

If you are interested in converting or renovating an existing building to flats or bedsits, you may be able to obtain a reduced VAT rate of 5 per cent on the costs of building and conversion materials.

Empty properties

Refurbishment or renovation of properties that have been empty for between 3 and 10 years attracts a VAT rate of 5 per cent, and properties that have been empty for over 10 years attract a zero VAT rate on refurbishment costs. You may need to obtain a certificate from your local authority confirming that the property is eligible. Contact the empty property officer at your local authority for more information.

DIY builders and converters refund scheme

If you are intending to build or convert your own property, or have this building or conversion done for you, it is possible to claim a VAT refund on your main construction or conversion costs. Rules and regulations are complex, and recent tribunals have complicated matters further. Therefore, you should seek professional advice if you are wishing to take advantage of this scheme.

Council tax

Council tax is payable on all dwellings in England, Wales and Scotland. These are defined as 'a separate unit of living accommodation, together with any garden, yard, garage or other outbuildings, attached to it, all occupied by the same person(s) and within the same area of land'. If a property contains more than one self-contained unit of accommodation, it will be divided into as many dwellings as there are self-contained units for council tax purposes. More information about council tax can be obtained from the Valuation Office Agency (details below).

Summary

As a potential property developer it is essential that you organize your finances carefully, making sure that you have enough capital to complete your project. This is of particular importance given the present economic conditions in the United Kingdom. Although mortgage companies are withdrawing some of their better mortgage deals and are less willing to lend to high-risk borrowers, there are still good mortgage deals available if you know where to look. An independent financial adviser will be able to offer advice about the best mortgages for your needs. You will be able to obtain a better mortgage deal, including buy-to-let mortgages, if you are able to pay a larger deposit. However, you must make sure that you have enough money to pay for your property development and to cover taxes such as SDLT and CGT.

To plan your business and understand your financial position, it is necessary to produce a comprehensive business plan, a profit/loss plan and a cash flow forecast. These issues are addressed in the next chapter.

Useful addresses

Institute of Chartered Accountants in England and Wales
Chartered Accountants' Hall, PO Box 433
London EC2P 2BJ
Tel: (020) 7920 8100
Fax: (020) 7920 0547
e-mail: generalenquiries@icaew.com
www.icaew.com
The Institute of Chartered Accountants sets and enforces standards of performance and conduct for chartered accountants in England and Wales. You can find a chartered accountant through the website.

Ethical Investment Research Service
80–84 Bondway
London SW8 1SF
Tel: (020) 7840 5700
Fax: (020) 7735 5323
e-mail: ethics@eiris.org
www.eiris.org
The Ethical Investment Research Service carries out independent research into corporate behaviour, providing information for people who want to invest ethically and helping them to make informed and responsible investment decisions. Independent financial advisers (IFAs) who offer ethical advice are listed in its online directory.

Ecology Building Society
7 Belton Road
Silsden, Keighley
West Yorkshire BD20 0EE
Tel: (0845) 674 5566
Fax: (01535) 650780
e-mail: info@ecology.co.uk
www.ecology.co.uk
The Ecology Building Society is a mutual organization which grants mortgages on properties and projects that help the environment. Its savings and mortgages are available across the United Kingdom. Details of its ecology mortgages and up-to-date mortgage rates are available on the website.

Useful websites

www.fsa.gov.uk
The Financial Services Authority (FSA) is the independent regulator set up by the government to look after the financial services industry and protect customers. On their website you can obtain information on financial planning, insurance, pensions, mortgages and warnings about scams, people and companies to avoid.

www.voa.gov.uk

The Valuation Office Agency is an executive agency of HM Revenue & Customs. It is responsible for compiling and maintaining the business rating and council tax lists for England and Wales. On the website you can obtain information about who pays the council tax, and find out the council tax band of a property in which you are interested. A helpline is available for enquiries: (0845 602 1507 in England; 0845 600 1748 in Wales).

Establishing your business

It is almost impossible for any type of business to survive without appropriate capital and financial planning. The previous chapter has offered advice on these issues. Once you know that you are able to secure the appropriate finances, you need to think more about what type of business you wish to run.

There are several ways to trade, and whichever method you choose will have implications for the way you run your business and the taxes that you pay. You will also need to produce a comprehensive business plan, profit/loss plan and cash flow forecast, and conduct a thorough risk assessment. This is especially important if you are hoping to receive financial backing for your business venture. This chapter offers further advice on establishing your business.

Deciding how to trade

Once you have assessed current economic conditions, thought about the type of property development in which you wish to invest, and have evaluated your skills and knowledge in relation to this, you need to think about how you are going to trade. There are three main ways of trading: as a sole trader, in a partnership or as a limited company. Different rules and regulations apply to each method of trading, and you should seek advice about the method most appropriate to your personal circumstances. As a general guide you can use the interactive tool on the Business Link website to find out which method of trading is suitable for your business (details below).

A sole trader

Setting up as a sole trader is the simplest and most common way of running a business, as there are fewer legal requirements involved and it does not require the payment of registration fees. However, as a sole trader you are ultimately personally liable for any losses your business makes, and creditors can pursue you for both business and personal assets. Your family home could be at risk if things go wrong, so you must carry out a thorough assessment of current economic and market conditions to determine whether your plans are sensible and viable.

If you decide to trade as a sole trader you will need to register with HM Revenue & Customs as self-employed. You will need to keep up-to-date books and records for tax purposes and submit an annual self-assessment tax return. More information and contact details of your local Inland Revenue Enquiry Centre can be obtained from www.hmrc.gov.uk.

A partnership

Setting up a partnership is similar to becoming a sole trader. Each partner will need to inform HM Revenue & Customs of his or her intention to become self-employed. Up-to-date accounts will need to be kept, and both individuals and the partnership will need to submit an annual self-assessment tax return.

A partnership does not have legal status. If one partner should withdraw from the business through bankruptcy, death or resignation, the partnership has to be dissolved, but the business may not need to cease. If you are thinking of following this route you should choose your partner very carefully, and obtain the services of a solicitor to draw up a contract. Agree terms that you both consider fair, and include a formula for breaking up, so that the relationship can remain amicable.

In a partnership both partners are personally liable for any debts incurred in the running of a business. However, it is possible to set up a limited liability partnership (LLP), which passes liability on to the partnership itself, rather than on to individuals. For more information about setting up an LLP contact Companies House (details below).

If you do decide to work with a partner, choose someone who is able to bring something useful to the partnership. This could be financial backing or knowledge and skills that you don't possess. However, you need to think carefully about going into business with friends and family. What would happen to your relationship if things go wrong?

Also, you need to think carefully about the work you and your partner are expected to do. 'Sleeping partners' who provide an initial cash outlay and then receive a share of the profits might initially seem a good idea. However, how will you feel in 10 years' time when you are working hard and your partner is doing nothing yet still receives a share of the profits?

A limited company

There are two main types of limited company. A private limited company is the most typical set-up for small businesses in the United Kingdom. It cannot offer shares to the public, but can have private shareholders. A public limited company, on the other hand, is permitted to sell shares to the public and raise funds in this way, although it must have issued shares to a value of at least £50,000 before it can trade.

Private limited companies must have at least one director, but do not have to have a company secretary. Public limited companies have to have at least two directors and a company secretary. You will need to choose a name for your company, file annual accounts at Companies House and produce corporate tax returns each year. Although legal requirements, rules, regulations and paperwork are more complex when setting up a limited company, your personal assets are safe in most cases. For more information about setting up a limited company, contact Companies House or consult the Business Link website (details below).

Developing a business plan

Developing a coherent business plan is important for any serious property investor. It covers all aspects of the development, from financial decisions to market research. When you develop your business plan, you need to consider all financial aspects in great detail. Even if your ideas for development are limited in duration, you still need to think very carefully about your finances and how they may be affected by current economic conditions (see Chapter 4).

If you want to succeed as a property developer you will need to carry out comprehensive market research (see Chapter 6). You will also need to think about your customers – potential buyers or potential tenants – and develop your property to meet their needs and expectations. Market research also involves finding out about your competitors. Never assume that you know best – your knowledge and experience will come in useful, but it needs to be backed up by comprehensive research and analysis.

Your business plan should contain the following sections:

- Summary – this should include an introduction to your plans and a financial overview.

- Management – who is to manage your business and what are their/your qualifications and experience?

- Key personnel – who will be involved in the business and what is their role?

- Product/service – this will include details of the property you intend to buy and what you intend to do with it in terms of letting or resale.

- Marketing – how do you intend to market your property, either to tenants or to buyers? Who are your competitors? What is your customer profile?

- Sales – what is the unique selling point? What advertising and promotion work do you expect to undertake? What are the costs of this work?

- Operational – what equipment will be required? Who is going to undertake the day-to-day running of the business? What are the costs involved?

- Short-term trading – what are your short-term objectives? What contingency plans do you have in place in case of problems such as a market crash or recession?

■ Financial documents – this will include your profit/loss plan and cash flow forecast. You should also include information about your contingency fund and details about how you intend to repay loans.

Producing a profit/loss plan and cash flow forecast

Before you take your plans and ideas to a financial backer, you will need to produce a profit/loss plan and a cash flow forecast. A profit/loss plan is a careful assessment of what you expect to happen with the income and expenditure of your business, and will help you to determine whether your project is viable.

For this plan you will have to familiarize yourself with the market and work out all the costs involved at the start of your project. This will include the price of the property, fees, materials and equipment, subcontracted work and labour. Then you need to work out how much you intend to make from sales or rent. The difference between the income from sales or rent and your direct costs is your gross profit (or loss).

You then need to think about how much it will cost to run your property business. This will include materials, equipment, transport, administration, insurance, promotion, professional expenses and interest on loans or mortgages. These are your overheads and are deducted from your gross profit. The figure you have left is your net profit (or loss).

From this profit/loss plan you can produce a cash flow forecast, which will show you how much money you need to set up and run your business. This forecast will also show you the areas of peak cash requirement through the year. A profit/loss plan and cash flow forecast may show that there are periods of loss during the year, but also periods of gain.

It is important to note that businesses fail because they are under-capitalized. Starting a business costs money, but experiencing losses also costs money, so you need to plan ahead to minimize potential loss. You also need to think about how you will cover running costs if you are unable to find tenants or sell your property. Also, what would happen if property prices fall so much that you experience negative equity on your property? Can you afford to change your investment strategy to a long-term plan so that you can wait until house prices rise again? More information about cash flow management can be obtained from the Business Link website (details below).

Conducting a risk assessment

Business is all about risk and commitment. Make sure that everybody understands the risks involved and is committed to making the business succeed. Before you set up your property business, carry out a risk assessment so that you are prepared for any problems that might arise and know how to deal with them before they escalate.

'Risk assessment' is a careful examination of what could go wrong and cause harm, whether this is physical, such as injuries and damage, or emotional, such as stress and anxiety. Carrying out a risk assessment in terms of health and safety issues is covered in depth in Chapter 18.

When conducting a risk assessment, think about the risks involved and the action required to reduce, manage or eliminate the risk, as shown in Table 5.1.

Through careful planning at the outset you will become more aware of what could go wrong with your property business, and you will be better able to tackle the problems when they arise. Some problems cannot be avoided, but if you are aware that these problems may occur, and you have appropriate insurance to cover yourself, you and/or your business will not suffer financially. Insurance issues are covered in depth in Chapter 14.

Summary

As a property investor you need to think about how you wish to trade, whether you are going to do so as a sole trader, in a partnership or as a limited company. It is important to produce a coherent and comprehensive business plan which includes a profit/loss plan and cash flow forecast. If you hope to obtain

Table 5.1 Risks and actions to reduce, manage or eliminate them

Risk	Action
Financial loss	Conduct thorough market research. Produce comprehensive profit/loss plan and cash flow forecast. Don't go over budget. Make sure appropriate finance is available. Develop appropriate financial skills.
Misunderstandings/ arguments	Plan and discuss everything thoroughly. Involve significant others. Negotiate/delegate appropriately. Obtain agreements in writing. Ensure all contracts are clear and legally binding.
Property damage	Obtain insurance. Develop appropriate DIY skills. Choose constructors carefully. Take appropriate care when working. Install fire doors/correctly fitting doors. Install smoke detectors. Choose tenants carefully. Don't leave property empty.
Personal injury	Carry out risk assessment. Learn and adhere to rules and regulations. Obtain appropriate insurance. Employ qualified, competent, insured workers.
Theft/burglary	Obtain insurance. Install appropriate security devices. Choose property and tenants carefully. Don't leave property empty.
Administrative problems	Install good equipment with anti-virus software. Develop appropriate skills or employ a skilled administrator. Back up records and store safely. Keep administration neat and orderly.

financial backing for your venture, you will need to make sure that you have these documents available.

Another essential aspect to the preparation and planning process is careful and thorough research. Without careful research your project could fail. These issues are discussed in the next chapter.

Useful addresses

Companies House
Crown Way, Maindy
Cardiff CF14 3UZ
Tel: (0870) 33 33 636
e-mail: enquiries@companies-house.gov.uk
www.companieshouse.gov.uk
The main functions of Companies House are to incorporate and dissolve limited companies, examine and store company information delivered under the Companies Act and make this information available to the public.

Useful websites

www.businesslink.gov.uk
This website provides practical advice for businesses, including information about how to trade, tax, employing people, and health and safety issues.

Stage Two
Progression

Doing your research

There are three basic principles involved in becoming a successful property developer: buy the right property, in the right location, at the right price. Given the current market conditions, a fourth principle can be added to this list: buy at the right time. Stick to these principles and your development should be successful. However, there are many issues involved in these points, and you will need to understand the property market and become familiar with the area and local prices before you are able to buy the right property, in the right location, at the right price, at the right time. This involves thorough and comprehensive research.

Advice on finding sources of information, conducting a price analysis, obtaining property information and conducting searches is offered in this chapter.

Finding sources of information

There are two main types of sources of information, primary sources and secondary sources. Obtaining information from primary sources involves first-hand observation and investigation, whereas secondary sources are studies that other people have made of a subject, such as research papers published in journals or on the internet. The different sources of property information are listed in Table 6.1.

Throughout this book you will be offered advice on obtaining information from the sources listed in Table 6.1. It is important to obtain information from as many different sources as possible, as this helps verify findings and increases your knowledge and understanding of the property market. Be aware of the reliability and validity of your source. If you are in any doubt about information you have collected, cross-reference with another source.

Table 6.1   Sources of property information

Primary sources	Secondary sources
Vendors	*Which?* reports
Neighbours	Mortgage company reports
Tenants	Financial newspapers and magazines
Landlords/associations	Property newspapers and magazines
Property developers	Social trends analyses
Builders	Local newspapers
Tradespeople	Local radio
Estate agents	Local and national television
Solicitors	Building society analyses
Conveyancers	Building Federation reports
Surveyors	Academic journals and reports
Census data	Government analyses and reports
Professional associations	Economic and market reviews
Mortgage lenders	Housing and property books
Land registers	Housing charity research
Citizens Advice Bureaux staff	
Council staff	
Planning applications	
Town/city development plans	
Yourself	
Your family	

Conducting a price analysis

Once you have decided that you wish to become a property developer you should start taking notice of what is happening with property prices in your area, or in the area in which you are interested. Monitor the prices and keep a record. This will help you to see how prices are changing, in both the short and long term. Regularly visit local estate agents and consult the local property press, again keeping records so that you can monitor changes.

As we have seen previously, house prices are falling in many parts of the United Kingdom and you need to keep an eye on these price changes so that you can understand how much they have dropped and make predictions about how much further they are likely to fall. This is useful research as it enables you to understand how long to wait before making an offer on a property so that you can receive the best bargain possible. You can find out how much house prices have fallen in all parts of the United Kingdom by consulting www.propertysnake.co.uk. You can search the site by postcode or area or look for a specific property. This website also shows how long a property has been on the market.

The Land Registry produces a *Residential Property Price Report*, which provides a detailed insight into what is happening to average prices and sales volumes in the residential property market for England and Wales. All sales are added together and an average price produced. This is useful on both a national and local level to get an up-to-date idea of house prices and sales. The information is freely available on the website (details below). A similar survey is produced in Scotland by the Registers of Scotland Executive Agency (details below).

The Department for Communities and Local Government produces a monthly house price index that is based on information supplied by mortgage lenders. Although it does not include cash purchases, it is a useful survey for getting a feel for what is happening in the housing market.

Both the Nationwide and the Halifax produce house price surveys that cover the entire United Kingdom. Again, these are based on property sales financed by mortgage lending and do not include cash sales, but they too provide a useful tool for finding out about house prices in the United Kingdom (details below).

Hometrack and Rightmove are two property websites that also produce their own house price surveys. Data are collected from estate agents throughout England and Wales who are asked to report on whether house prices are rising or falling. This does not reflect the price at which properties actually sell, but again it is a useful tool for finding out more about what is happening with house prices (details below).

Obtaining property information

Find out which local and national newspapers have property sections that advertise property in the area in which you are interested. Check relevant websites as this information may be available online.

Using the internet

Using the internet can be the quickest and easiest way to obtain property information. There are a vast number of property websites now available, covering properties in the United Kingdom and overseas. Some of these websites are run by estate agents, whereas others have been set up for people who wish to advertise their property independently. Always check the 'about us' section to find out more about the organization, and never hand over money or personal details if you have any doubt or suspicion about the site.

Many of the property websites will not provide a map or the address of the property for security reasons. However, once you have found out the postcode or the location of the property, you can obtain a map by consulting www.multimap.com or maps.google.co.uk, from which you can also obtain a satellite image of the area. This is useful for providing an instant visual representation of the place in which the property is situated. This may alert you to potential problems such as a major road or railway running beside the property.

Using estate agents

When using an estate agent you should find out whether it is registered with the National Association of Estate Agents (NAEA) or the Ombudsman for Estate Agents (OEA). Members of both organizations have to adhere to a code of practice and agree to being judged by a third party if a complaint is made. This should help to protect your rights as a customer. You can access contact details of members from the relevant websites (details below).

Estate agents are useful for obtaining information about how the property market is performing in their area. However, you should always check the validity and reliability of the information you have received by using other sources. Remember that estate agents' job is to sell property, and their enthusiasm for this may have an influence on the information they supply.

You can register online with many estate agents, and they will e-mail details of relevant properties. Give specific criteria. You can alter, update or cancel these at any time. Be selective about the companies to whom you give your e-mail address, and make sure they do not pass on your details to other organizations unless they have your permission.

Using auction houses

If you are interested in buying at auction, visit your local estate agents and ask them whether they know of local auctions in the area. Some of the larger estate agents work closely with auctioneers and will provide information about contacting local auction houses or a booklet or DVD that explains the process of buying property at auction. Ask to be put on the auction house mailing list and they will then send you their catalogues for auctions that are to take place in your area. It is possible to find out about auctions in your area from the internet, but most sites will require you to register and pay a fee, whereas information from estate agents is free for potential purchasers.

There is potential to obtain a greater bargain at auction because many mortgage companies use auction houses to dispose of properties that have been repossessed or properties that are in need of considerable improvement and modernization. However, if you choose this option you have to make sure that you do not get carried away with your bidding, and hope that a bidding war does not occur on the property in which you are interested. More information about buying at auction is provided in Chapter 11.

Conducting property searches

When searching for properties think about doing so out of the peak selling season, which tends to be spring and summer. People are less keen on selling in autumn and winter. This means that, in many cases, people who are selling at this time of year have to do so for a reason, such as relocating for work or a lender needing to sell a property that has been repossessed. This may mean that they are looking for a quick sale and are more willing to be flexible on offers you make.

Developing a search checklist

When you begin your search you may find it useful to develop a checklist which will help you to narrow down your search and only hunt for suitable properties in the appropriate locations. Your checklist will depend on the type of development in which you are interested. An example of such a checklist is provided in Table 6.2.

You can provide estate agents with a copy of the list and ask that they only send you details of relevant properties.

Summary

All successful property developers realize the importance of undertaking thorough and comprehensive research. Through careful research you will be able to develop a deeper understanding of the property market, both locally and nationally. This will help you to avoid many of the pitfalls associated with property development, especially if property prices continue to fall.

Once you have conducted this background research you can start to think about the more specific details of your search. The next chapter offers advice about choosing the right location and avoiding areas with potential investment problems.

Table 6.2 Checklist example

Maximum price:	£150,000
Location:	Leicester, close to university
Desired date of purchase:	ASAP
Property type:	Terraced
Minimum no. of bedrooms:	4
Essential house features:	Must have 4 or more bedrooms Must be desirable to students Must be structurally sound
Essential location features:	Within walking distance of university

Investment potential:

▌ Is it cheap to buy?

▌ Will it be cheap to refurbish?

▌ Will it be easy to let?

▌ Will I be able to let the property in the summer?

▌ Will students be willing to pay a retainer over the summer?

▌ Is there competition for student property, so I can let it early in the year and know that I have tenants before the start of the academic year?

▌ Are house prices rising in the area?

▌ Are houses sold quickly in the area?

▌ Is it a popular location with students?

▌ Would non-students buy in that area?

▌ Will I be able to sell on if I need to?

Useful addresses

National Association of Estate Agents
Arbon House
6 Tournament Court
Warwick CV34 4EH
Tel: (01926) 496800
Fax: (01926) 417788
e-mail: info@naea.co.uk
www.naea.co.uk
The National Association of Estate Agents (NAEA) is the largest professional estate agency organization in the United Kingdom. All members must operate to a professional code of practice and rules of conduct. You can obtain contact details of registered estate agents on the website and search for properties in your desired location.

Ombudsman for Estate Agents
Beckett House
4 Bridge Street
Salisbury, Wilts SP1 2LX
Tel: (01722) 333306
Fax: (01722) 332296
e-mail: admin@oea.co.uk
www.oea.co.uk
The Ombudsman for Estate Agents (OEA) has been established to provide a free, fair and independent service to buyers and sellers of residential property in the United Kingdom. On the website you can access information about members and the results of housing surveys.

Useful websites

www.landregistry.gov.uk
On this site you can find out about average house prices throughout England and Wales, narrowing your search to specific postcode areas. If you are interested in finding out more about a specific property there is a small fee for the service.

www.ros.gov.uk
This is the website of the Registers of Scotland Executive Agency.
It provides information about Scotland's land and property. On
the website, for a small fee, you can find out about property prices
anywhere in Scotland.

www.hbosplc.com
This is the website of the merged Halifax and Bank of Scotland.
Details of the Halifax House Price Index can be found on this
website. The survey is useful for providing national and regional
house prices and for showing quarterly and annual changes in
house prices. You are able to click on the relevant region of the
United Kingdom to find out more information about that area.

www.nationwide.co.uk
The Nationwide house prices survey can be found on this
website. There is also a useful calculator that enables you to find
out how the price of a property in which you are interested has
changed over the past few years. Again, this survey is useful for
providing information about how house prices have changed in
the different regions of the United Kingdom.

www.hometrack.co.uk
Hometrack provides an in-depth and up-to-date survey of house
prices in England and Wales. The website contains useful information on house price growth, time to sell, affordability, mortgage
lending and repossessions, in addition to interesting commentary
and analysis concerning the state of the housing market.

www.nethouseprices.com
This website provides a useful search tool for finding house
prices in particular locations throughout England, Scotland and
Wales. The information is based on information recorded by the
Land Registry and the Registers of Scotland. The service is free
to use, though you are required to register before you receive
your quotation.

www.mouseprice.co.uk
This website provides information to house buyers, sellers and professionals about house prices in the United Kingdom. You can search by location and receive selling prices for houses in that area over the past few years.

www.rightmove.co.uk
You can find details of the Rightmove.co.uk House Price Index on this website. The service is free to use and provides useful commentary and analysis on housing market trends.

7 Recognizing potential locations

Once you have considered prices in the area in which you are interested and you have worked out that you can afford to buy in this particular area, you need to consider whether it is a good place to buy property for investment purposes. Although it might seem a good deal in the short term, you also need to think about the long-term development prospects and the investment potential of the location.

This chapter offers advice about choosing the right location, from recognizing areas of regeneration and degeneration, to choosing sites that will be suitable for your development and investment plans.

Recognizing property hot spots

Recognizing property hot spots can be quite simple in the United Kingdom. There are a variety of programmes on television and radio, property magazines, journals and newspapers, organizations and professionals who are willing to offer advice about the best places to buy in the United Kingdom. Take note of this advice as it can complement your personal research.

In addition to this advice, there are other clues available to indicate that a location is doing well and could be considered a property hot spot:

- Aggressive selling by estate agents, owners and investors – although this may also happen in property black spots, this behaviour tends to indicate a confidence in the market, especially when you take into account the other clues listed below.

- New estate agents springing up in the town/city centre with lower estate agent fees as they compete for custom.

- Increasing property advertising in local newspapers and by flyers through doors.

- Evidence of large- and small-scale development in the area, by private developers and the local authority.

- A buoyant and fast-moving property market.

- 'For sale' or 'to let' signs in the whole area can be a positive sign, but be wary of small pockets of these signs as they could indicate a forthcoming development which residents feel will have a negative impact on their property price. However, don't discount such an area. Local residents may be thinking about the short-term disruption to their peace and quiet and may not be thinking about the long-term potential of the development.

It is one thing to be able to recognize an existing property hot spot, but it is another to predict where the next property hot spot is likely to be. Once a location has been mentioned by the media or professionals, many of the bargains will already have been snapped up by savvy property investors. To join these investors you need to predict which areas are going to become property hot spots before everyone else knows about them. One of the ways to do this is to recognize the signs of urban regeneration and degeneration.

Spotting areas of regeneration

For the past 15 years urban regeneration policy in the United Kingdom has been marked by a growing emphasis on community involvement. When choosing an area, look for signs of this involvement. Communities that work together with thriving social networks tend to look after the area in which they live. This type of location can also be a magnet for like-minded families who are prepared to pay more to live in an area that they perceive to be friendly and safe for bringing up children.

The following signs provide an indication that a location is in the process of being regenerated:

▌ New development on land that was previously unpopular, such as old petrol stations, wasteland and areas near to railway tracks. New housing development figures can be obtained from your local authority planning department.

▌ Signs of 'gentrification' – this is the gradual conversion of less desirable and developed areas into much more fashionable areas. It tends to be young professionals and young families who move into these areas, desiring to be close to their work place and wanting to buy a home with period features.

▌ New bars, coffee shops, art studios and independent specialist food shops and cafés opening in the city and town centre.

▌ Greater and more sophisticated leisure and entertainment facilities – theatres, gyms, nightclubs and small music venues.

▌ Rapid growth in the local business sector.

▌ Expensive cars parked in driveways.

▌ Improved building façades and landscaping of front gardens and driveways. Less property 'letting down' the street.

When considering areas of regeneration, look to surrounding areas that might still appear run-down but might become popular once the adjacent area becomes fully developed and regenerated. These areas can provide more potential for your development if you are prepared to take the risk and invest over the long term.

Avoiding areas of over-development

Over the last decade there has been a massive increase in the number of city centre developments as property developers, driven on by vastly inflated property prices, have taken advantage of tax incentives for the development and conversion of city centre buildings. However, many are now struggling to sell or let their properties, mainly due to falling house prices, over-supply and lack of demand for this type of property. As a new property developer you should be very wary of this type of development, given the current economic position. Also, some mortgage companies are not willing to lend on certain city centre apartments. Even if this type of area seems to be undergoing regeneration, you need to find out how quickly properties sell or are let, whether there is still a market available and whether it is possible to make money on this type of development in that location.

Speak to local developers and builders, join the local landlords group and contact your local planning authority. Approach local estate agents and letting agents, monitor sales prices and find out the amount of time that it takes for a property to sell. Find out if any of the properties have been repossessed by obtaining more details about those that come onto the market. Although estate agents are reluctant to advertise that a property is a repossession, they will pass on this information when pushed, if you show that you are a serious buyer or if you are able to establish a trusting relationship with your local agent. Auction houses tend to use the term 'by order of mortgagee' when describing a property that has been repossessed, although again, some will not supply this information in the catalogue for fear of putting off potential purchasers.

Spotting areas of degeneration

There are certain places in the United Kingdom that you should avoid if you want to make money on your investment. In general, and unless you have a really strong belief that the area will eventually improve, you should avoid purchasing in locations with the following signs of degeneration:

- fewer homes on the market and properties taking longer and longer to sell;

- less advertising by estate agents, homeowners and investors and estate agents closing down;

- shops, bars and cafés going out of business or closing down;

- increasing problems with broken windows, boarded properties and empty properties;

- an increasing number of run-down properties, unkempt gardens and boundaries;

- increasing problems with abandoned cars;

- increasing problems with litter, graffiti and vandalism;

- rising crime levels and higher levels of policing;

- little evidence of community involvement or social networking;

- increasing reports of crime and drug/alcohol abuse.

Choosing suitable locations

When choosing a suitable location you must have your business plan in mind, as this will help you to think about the right location for the type of development in which you are interested (see Chapter 5). For example, desirable properties for tenants are conveniently located for public transport, local amenities, restaurants and bars, and have private parking facilities. However, a family looking to buy a property may wish to be well away from the hustle and bustle of city centre life and choose somewhere that they perceive to have thriving community involvement.

In addition to taking into account your business plan, there are some general questions that you should ask for all types of property development, whether you intend to live in the property yourself, let it to tenants, or sell to someone else:

- Would you live in the area? Would you feel comfortable and safe doing so?

- Is the local economy thriving, driven primarily by the private sector, but with public sector spending in evidence?

- Is the property convenient for local shops and transport?

- Is there free parking?

- Are there any restrictions placed on planning and development?

If you are intending to improve or develop the property in any way, this last point is very important. Find out whether there are any general restrictions on your plans before you waste time, effort and money on buying a property in an area unsuitable for your development. These restrictions could include greenfield sites (see below) and conservation areas (see Chapter 8).

Knowing about redfield, brownfield and greenfield sites

The type of site on which the property is situated has implications for the type of development you may be able to undertake. The three main types are redfield, brownfield and greenfield sites.

Redfield sites

The new term of 'redfield site' has been introduced recently because some people believe that the term 'brownfield' is too broad and has not been well defined. Redfield is taken to mean the conversion of existing buildings to provide housing, and includes returning empty homes to use, conversions of redundant commercial buildings and better use of existing buildings.

Throughout the United Kingdom there are thousands of empty, disused and run-down properties of this type. Environmental groups such as the Campaign to Protect Rural England (CPRE) believe that some of the United Kingdom's housing problems could be solved by doing more to encourage urban regeneration and through better use of existing buildings (details below). They are urging the government to offer more incentives to developers. This is an area of property development that could become much more significant over the next few years once the property market settles, with more grants and incentives becoming available.

Brownfield sites

Brownfield sites are any land or premises that have previously been used but are not fully in use now, though they may be partially utilized or occupied. The land may be vacant, derelict or contaminated. Some brownfield sites cannot be used without some type of intervention, especially if the land has been contaminated in any way or damaged by industrial use. Brownfield sites can be found in city and town centres, residential areas, former industrial areas and former mining areas.

Local planning authorities must demonstrate an up-to-date five-year supply of 'deliverable' sites for housing, a list of specific, developable sites for the next 6 to 10 years and a further list of sites, or areas for broad growth, for the next 11 to 15 years. Sixty per cent of this land must come from previously developed areas. Local planning authorities are required to prove that this is happening on an annual basis. This means that they will be keen to identify suitable brownfield sites and may look more favourably on planning applications for this type of site. However, if you are interested in following this route, you need to be aware of the following points:

- Not all brownfield land is suitable for housing. This can be because of inadequate access or large industrial use close by.

- The decontamination process can be complicated, costly and time-consuming. It may be viable only for large-scale developers.

- Local residents who remember the site may be unwilling to live there. However, if your site is chosen carefully, there is scope for encouraging outsiders who do not have negative memories of the site.

- It may be harder to obtain insurance for damaged or contaminated land.

- A full survey of the site will be needed to obtain planning permission. This will include: the physical characteristics of the site such as topography and the ground-bearing capacity for foundations; environmental issues such as existing trees, flora, fauna and water features; in-site issues such as noise, traffic generation and waste disposal; and the history of the site, such as previous use and archaeological remains. This is in addition to your plans for the building(s).

These points illustrate why you should think carefully about developing a brownfield site. You should seek the appropriate advice, and conduct thorough and careful research if you decide to follow this route.

Greenfield sites

'Greenfield' refers to land that has not previously been used for building or manufacturing. These sites can be located in both urban and rural areas, and include forestry, agricultural and park land. A common misconception is that developers cannot build on greenfield sites. This is not the case – throughout the United Kingdom, greenfield sites are being developed on a large scale, and there is widespread concern from environmentalists that too many greenfield sites are being used for property development.

Greenfield sites are obviously popular because of their huge potential. They are not contaminated, they tend to be located away from industry, and they might be scenic, tranquil areas in which expensive property can be built. However, you should think carefully about whether you want to develop on a greenfield site as this land is disappearing rapidly, planning permission will be hard to obtain, and you will face a long fight from campaign groups. For advice about developing alternative sites and protecting greenfield land, consult the CPRE (details below).

Summary

Choosing the right location is an important part of successful property development. If you are unfamiliar with an area in which you wish to buy, you must undertake comprehensive and thorough research before you make your purchase. Time spent during this preparation stage will reduce problems at a later date. There are many issues you should consider when choosing a location. These include issues of regeneration, degeneration and matching suitability to your customers and/or tenants.

Once you have conducted your location research, you need to look into the development and investment potential of the area in which you are interested. These issues are discussed in the next chapter.

Useful addresses

Campaign to Protect Rural England
128 Southwark Street
London SE1 0SW
Tel: (020) 7981 2800
Fax: (020) 7981 2899
e-mail: info@cpre.org.uk
www.cpre.org.uk
The Campaign to Protect Rural England (CPRE) 'exists to promote the beauty, tranquillity and diversity of rural England by encouraging the sustainable use of land and other natural resources in town and country'. If you are hoping to become a property developer but are concerned about the possible impact on the countryside, you can seek advice from this organization. The website contains useful information about government housing policy and its impact on rural England.

8 **Recognizing potential for development**

Once you have found the right property in the right location, you need to think about the development potential of the property. This involves a careful analysis of the local market, in terms of letting potential and resale value. It also involves an analysis of the competition and a consideration of the short- and long-term development potential.

However, even if your analyses suggest that this is the right property, in the right location, at the right price, and that now is the right time to buy, you also need to find out whether there is anything that would restrict or stop your plans for development. This includes restrictions on development in the area and restrictions on development of the individual property. These issues are discussed in this chapter.

Researching the development system and planning control

Development is controlled by the local planning authority (LPA), which is usually the district or borough council. Its role is to ensure that development takes place when it is needed, but that the character and amenities within the area are not adversely affected by the development.

If your property is located in a region that has a unitary authority, it will deal with all planning issues. In areas with a two- or three-tier system of local authority, the district and/or borough council deals with local planning matters. It prepares a local plan for its area and deals with most of the planning applications. The county council prepares a structure plan for the area. Although it does not tend to deal with individual planning applications, it is useful to find out what is being planned for the future in terms of waste, development, regeneration, pollution and so on.

Local authorities have to follow national guidelines on managing development in their area, although specific rules, procedures and conditions apply locally. It is important, therefore to become familiar with the procedures in the area in which you intend to buy a property.

Many local authorities now publish details of their planning frameworks and strategies in the 'Planning services' or 'Environment and planning' section of their website. This is the easiest and quickest way to access the information. If this information is unavailable on the website, contact the planning department of your local authority to find out how you can access the information.

The planning register is open for inspection, at no charge, in every local authority office. This lists all recent and current planning applications by a reference number that is also noted on an Ordnance Survey map of the area. This shows you the type of development that has been given planning consent or been refused, and the areas in which the development is situated. You can also obtain information about the applicants and their agents from this register. This is useful if you are new to an area, as it provides useful addresses of developers who will be able to offer advice about local development issues.

If you are interested in buying property in other parts of the country you can obtain information about development plans in most areas by visiting the Government's Planning Portal (www.planningportal.gov.uk). This enables you to enter the postcode of the area in which you are interested and view the development plan for that area. Through this portal you can access useful information about development and building control, and regional and county planning issues, and view a weekly planning register for the area in which you are interested.

Understanding restrictions on development

Some properties will have restrictions placed on them in terms of the development that can be undertaken. Some of these are because of the particular type of property, whereas others are to do with the area in which the property is located. The most common types of restriction are placed on listed buildings, properties in sensitive areas and through covenants in the title deeds.

Listed buildings

Development on listed buildings is restricted, so you should think carefully before buying a listed building. If you want to alter a listed building in any way, inside or out, you must find out whether you need listed building consent. This is in addition to any planning permission that may be required. It is an offence to undertake any of this work without the appropriate consent.

Before you consider buying a listed building for your development project you should speak to the conservation officer at your local council to find out whether your plans are likely to be accepted. This will avoid you wasting time, effort and money. If you decide to go ahead you will need to work with an architect who is experienced in listed building works. An application form can be obtained from your local authority, and you will need to include all required information such as photographs, plans and drawings with your application. It usually takes at least eight weeks for a decision to be made and if consent is refused you have six months in which to lodge an appeal.

If you own a listed building and the local authority feels that you are not conducting the necessary repairs or preserving the building in an appropriate manner, it can serve a repair notice on you. If the required work is not carried out within two months it is possible for the local authority to make a compulsory purchase order on the property. For more information about listed buildings consult the English Heritage website: www.english-heritage.org.uk.

Sensitive areas

Development is often restricted in sensitive parts of the country. These include the following areas:

- conservation areas;
- national parks;
- designated areas of outstanding natural beauty.

Information about sensitive areas can be obtained from the local authority in which the property is located. Most keep maps that can be inspected by the public. If you find that a property falls within a sensitive area, you should discuss your plans informally with a planning officer before making your purchase. In some cases local authorities are very strict about the type of work that can be undertaken, and you will be able to find out whether your ideas are likely to receive approval before making a purchase (see Chapter 12). To find out more about areas of outstanding natural beauty in England and Wales, contact the National Association for Areas of Outstanding Natural Beauty (details below).

Restrictive covenants

These may be placed on buildings in new developments to control building work so that unsightly or out-of-place alterations are not carried out. If you are thinking of buying a property on a new estate, you should check first whether the developer has imposed any such restrictions. Since most covenants are included in the title deeds of a property, this issue is covered in more depth in Chapter 11.

Analysing the local market

Think about the local market in terms of development potential. What other development is going on in the area, both by the local authority and by private developers? Look for signs of building work – scaffolding, cranes, skips and mixers. Approach some of the builders and find out what is going on. Most will be happy to talk to you if you show an interest in what they are doing.

Consider the current market – is it buoyant? Are there plenty of estate agents in the area with strong advertising strategies? Discuss the market with estate agents to find out what is happening currently in the area, and discuss their predictions for the future. How have house prices changed over the past few years, and how do estate agents expect them to change in the future, especially given current market conditions? Consult house price surveys for more information (see Chapter 5).

Speak to planning officers and view development plans held by the local authority. Find out what development is planned for the near future and how officers feel this will affect the local area.

If you are interested in buying a property to let, find out how many other properties of a similar type are available in the area. Speak to local letting agents and find out about current trends and future prospects. Scan local newspapers to find out about the type of property that is being advertised and the levels of rent being charged.

Think about the type of tenants you wish to attract, and speak to relevant people or organizations. For example, if you are thinking about providing property for students, arrange an appointment with the accommodation officer at the local college and/or university. Find out what these people think about the rental market in the area. Or if you are thinking about corporate lets, make contact with some of the larger businesses to find out whether they would require accommodation for their employees, and whether they think the market could sustain more private rented accommodation in the area.

Analysing the competition

If you are intending to let your property, you need to find out about the competition. In particular, you need to conduct an analysis of the type and quantity of rented property in the area, and make sure that saturation point has not been reached. You also need to find out about the market for private rented accommodation. Who are the potential tenants and how many are available?

When you conduct your analysis, think about whether the local area can sustain more private rented accommodation. Even if saturation point has been reached there may be a possibility of your entering the market if you have something unique, different or of value to potential tenants. However, to find whether this is the case you need to conduct thorough research and make sure you have confidence in the market before you make your purchase.

In the housing section of the Communities and Local Government website you can obtain information about the tenure of housing in specific locations, including up-to-date tables about local authority and privately rented accommodation (details below). This will give you a general picture of the type of housing tenure in the area. Next, make contact with local landlord associations and letting agents. Get to know which organizations are operating in the area, what type of accommodation they provide and how easy it is to find tenants.

Networking is important. If you get to know other landlords you may be able to visit their properties and speak to some of their existing tenants. To do this you need to foster an atmosphere of cooperation rather than competition.

Recognizing short- and long-term potential

Predicting the future is impossible. However, you can gain a deeper understanding of what might happen in the future by looking at what has happened in the past and how this influences the current housing market (see Chapter 1). The recent boom may be over, and house prices in some parts of the country are falling. However, there are still good development opportunities available, and this will always be the case.

When considering the short- and/or long-term potential of an investment, think about what is happening in the local area in terms of regeneration or degeneration (see Chapter 7). It is obvious that you would not spend a lot of your money, time and effort renovating a property in an area that is run down and exhibiting signs of degeneration, rather than regeneration over the next few years. However, some run-down areas are now showing signs of regeneration, so a long-term investment in that type of area could provide considerable profit on your investment.

There are many different ways to invest in property. Some developers decide to utilize short-term investment opportunities, whereas others are concerned about the long-term potential. However, as we have seen previously, you need to be wary of short-term opportunities in today's economic climate (see Chapter 1). Also, some locations are better for short-term investment, whereas others are better over the long term. Often the long-term investment opportunities provide greater potential in terms of profit, but they might come with greater risks attached. Personal circumstances, available finances, motivation, interests, economic conditions and location will all have an influence on your decision concerning the length of investment.

If you are interested in obtaining a buy-to-let mortgage and letting your property, you will need to think about this as a long-term investment. Although it is possible to obtain a loan for a shorter period of time, the repayments will probably exceed your rental income, and most lenders will be unwilling to lend large amounts of money in these circumstances.

Refurbishing or renovating a property provides the opportunity for shorter-term investment if you intend to sell the property after you have completed the work. However, if you hope to obtain a mortgage on this type of property you will have to be in a very secure financial position and be able to convince the lender that it is a viable project with profit potential. You will also have to convince the lender of your competence and reliability to carry out the required work, and be prepared to pay significant arrangement fees. Also, you will have to display a thorough understanding of how the market is performing over the short term and the influence this will have on your investment.

Finding out about ownership

Before you buy a property for development, you need to consider the type of ownership of the property. In England and Wales there are three types of ownership: freehold, leasehold and common-hold. A freehold property is where you own both the property and the land on which it is built. The buyer of a leasehold property owns the property for a set number of years, but does not own the land on which it stands. More information about leasehold can be obtained from the Leasehold Advisory Service (details below).

Commonhold is a form of land ownership that was introduced in 2004. This system relates to blocks of flats and other buildings made up of individual units. In the building each unit is held as freehold and the common parts of the building are held and managed by a Commonhold Association. This is a private limited company of which the unit holders are members. This system has been devised to get rid of leasehold in blocks of flats, but as conversion to the new system is not compulsory, the two exist side by side. In theory it is possible for owners of flats in a block on which you hold the freehold to convert their ownership to commonhold. However, in practice this would be difficult and costly, requiring the agreement and cooperation of all leaseholders.

The type of ownership on a property has implications for the type of development you are able to undertake. Look into this carefully before making purchasing decisions. For example, leasehold properties may come with restrictive covenants that will influence what building work you can undertake, and you may not be able to sublet the property.

Summary

Before you can start your development project you need to undertake a careful analysis of the market, which includes a consideration of the existing stock and the availability of potential tenants in the area. Careful and thorough analysis will help to avoid problems later on in your project. You also need to consider any restrictions on development. These will include the type of ownership of the property, covenants and the status of the building and the area in which it is located.

Once you have satisfied yourself of the viability of the project in a particular area, you can go on to view specific properties. Advice for viewing a property is offered in the next chapter.

Useful addresses

Leasehold Advisory Service
31 Worship Street
London EC2A 2DX
Tel: (020) 7374 5380
Fax: (020) 7374 5373
e-mail: info@lease-advice.org.uk
www.lease-advice.org.uk
The Leasehold Advisory Service provides free advice on the law affecting residential long-leasehold property and commonhold property.

The National Association for Areas of Outstanding Natural Beauty
The Old Police Station, Cotswold Heritage Centre
Northleach
Gloucestershire GL54 3JH
Tel: (01451) 862007
Fax: (01451) 862001
e-mail: jill.smith@cotswoldsaonb.org.uk
www.aonb.org.uk
The National Association for Areas of Outstanding Natural Beauty (NAAONB) is an independent organization formed in 1998 to act on behalf of areas of outstanding natural beauty in England and Wales. On its website you can view a map of all these areas and obtain local contact details and useful geographical information about each area.

Useful websites

www.communities.gov.uk
On this website you can access information about housing tenure in England and Wales, including information about private tenancies and levels of rent, registered fair rents and private tenancies by type.

Stage Three
Procurement

Viewing a property

When you have found a property in which you are interested, you need to inspect it in detail, planning your visit carefully and recording pertinent information for future reference. It is important to be organized before you begin your viewing. If you know what to look for in advance, your visit will be more productive and worthwhile.

This chapter offers advice about planning your viewing, asking questions, making observations, developing a checklist and avoiding problem properties.

Organizing your viewing

When you begin to arrange your viewing, it is important to be organized from the outset, especially if you intend to view a number of properties. Keep a file on each property so that you can easily reference each of them when required. This will include the property details, your observation checklist (see below) and any other information relevant to the property, such as surveyors' reports, planning applications and so on, which should be included in the Home Information Pack. This written record provides a useful resource to which to return when comparing prices, standard of property and potential for development.

Never make a decision on one viewing. Always return to a property at a different time of day and on a different day of the week. Make sure that you visit a property during the day and during the evening, on a weekday and at the weekend. If the vendors are serious about selling their property, and if they know you are a serious potential purchaser, they will not mind arranging extra viewings for you.

Also, drive by the property when the vendor is not expecting you to check whether anything is different and might have been altered for your viewing. Have a look at the neighbouring properties and check to see whether there might be any potential problems.

Talk to neighbours. Often it is useful to talk to those opposite or those a little further along the road, as they might have some interesting information to provide. Don't ask directly about the property, but discuss the area, the sense of community, local campaigns and so on. Once you have struck up a conversation you can ask more specific questions about the property and close neighbours. (Researching the neighbourhood is discussed in more depth in Chapter 10.)

Questioning the vendor or selling agent

Before you undertake a viewing, think about how you can question the vendor or selling agent to elicit the type of information you require. Be aware that people don't always tell the truth. One way that you can get around this problem is to ask the same question in different ways. Also, you could try asking the same question separately to two people selling the house if possible. Sometimes it may be preferable to ask this type of question via the telephone when you are only talking to one person.

Listen carefully to the answers you are being given, watching eye movement and body language. If someone looks 'shifty', and doesn't make eye contact when answering your questions, the chances are that he or she has something to hide. Take a mental note of the question and try to find out more information for yourself, using different sources. For example, a vendor might not want to mention recent flood damage, but neighbours three doors away might be more than happy to tell you of their experiences during the floods.

Some useful questions to ask the vendor are:

▌ Why are you selling the property?

▌ Where are you moving to?

▌ How do you get on with the neighbours?

- Is the property freehold? If not, how much is the ground rent and how many years are left on the lease?

- Are there any restrictions placed on what you can do within the property and grounds?

- Does anyone have the right to cross the property boundaries?

- Are there any communal areas within the property boundaries? If so, who is responsible for their maintenance?

- Are there any restrictions placed on running a business from the property? Are there any restrictions to you putting up a sign, plaque or parking your business van on the premises?

- Is there vacant possession on the property? If you are intending to let the property and it already has tenants, you need to think carefully about whether you will keep the same tenants. Find out how long they have been in the property and what type of contract they have signed. Try to meet the tenants and have a chat with them. You should note, however, that mortgage lenders tend to be reluctant to offer mortgages on tenanted properties.

- Has the property ever been flooded or faced risk from flooding?

- Are there any restrictions placed on the owner making alterations or developing the property?

- Has the property been altered in any way, and if so, does the vendor have copies of the relevant planning and building control consents for you to inspect? If it is a listed building, do they have the relevant listed building consent for any work undertaken? If they cannot produce this information you should be wary about buying this type of property as, if the authorities find out that unauthorized work has been carried out, you could be liable to put the building back to the way it was at your own expense.

- Has the house been protected against damp? Does it have a damp-proof course? Does the vendor have a guarantee on the work?

■ If the property has any flat roofs, does the vendor know when they were replaced? (In general, felt roofs last about 10 years, asphalt roofs up to 30 years and good fibreglass roofs will last over 30 years.)

■ What is included in the sale?

Some of this information will be included in the home information pack (see Chapter 21).

Using overt and covert observation techniques

There are two main types of observation technique: covert and overt. Covert observation means that what you are doing is under cover – no one knows who you are and that you are doing your research. Overt observation means that people are aware of your presence and your purpose.

When you view a property the vendor and/or estate agent know that you are there to look at the property and decide whether or not it is the right place for you. If they really want to sell the property they will try to do what they can to convince you that the property would be a good purchase. This means that positive aspects are exaggerated and negative aspects minimized or ignored.

As a potential purchaser, it is up to you to make sure that you receive the correct balance between positive and negative aspects. Since you cannot rely on the vendor or estate agent to disclose this information, you must find out for yourself. You need to develop and improve your overt and covert observation skills so that you can find out as much as possible about your potential purchase.

Observation involves using the senses of smell, sight, sound and touch. When you a view a property you can use all these senses to get a feel for the property, its structure and the local community and neighbourhood. If you observe well, using all these senses together, the vendor may not be aware of what you are doing.

Sense of smell

▌ Does the property smell damp? If it does there might be problems with dry or wet rot.

▌ Can you notice any other unusual smells that you can't place? Ventilation could be the problem. Has the chimney breast been blocked up? Do all the windows open?

▌ Do the drains smell, inside or outside the property? This could indicate blockages, inadequate drainage or more serious problems with the sewage system in the local area.

▌ Can you smell coffee, baking bread or cakes? If you can, is the vendor using an old trick to try to cover bad smells?

Sense of sight

▌ Can you see any problems with the structure of the property? Are there any cracks on brickwork outside and/or on plaster inside? Does the roof bow? Are walls straight? Is plaster bubbling? Are there gaps between the floorboards and skirting boards?

▌ Is wallpaper peeling? This could indicate a problem with damp.

▌ What can you see in the local neighbourhood and surrounding properties? Are there any eyesores? Is there anything blocking views from the windows or from the garden?

▌ Have you seen the neighbours? Do they look like the sort of people with whom you, or your tenants, would be happy to be neighbours?

▌ Can you spot any potential building work or development that would affect the value of the property, either positively or negatively?

Sense of sound

▌ Can you hear any noises that might be annoying or disturb your peace, or that of your tenants? Try to visit a property at different times and on different days so that you can find out how noise levels might vary through the day and week. If the vendors have music on, ask them to switch it off, in case they are hiding something.

■ Can you hear floorboards and stairs creaking? This may indicate some type of rot or decay.

■ Can you hear any unusual noises from the boiler or radiators? If so, ask the vendor to explain them. Ask to see previous bills and find out when the boiler was last serviced.

Sense of touch

■ Does any woodwork crumble when you run your hands along it? This indicates rot and decay.

■ Can you feel any lumps and bumps in plaster, under wallpaper, through carpets?

■ Are hot-water taps and radiators efficient and warm enough? Ask the vendor to demonstrate.

■ Do any walls feel damp?

Developing a checklist

It is useful to develop an observation checklist as it will help to remind you of all the important information of which you should be taking notice. Also, if you are viewing a number of properties, it provides a useful source of reference.

In the checklist in Figure 9.1, you should try to tick as many 'yes' answers as possible. A derelict or empty property might not score too highly on this checklist, but the higher the better as this will reduce the amount of work you will have to undertake on the property, should you decide to purchase. If you miss anything important on the first viewing, make sure you find the answer on the second viewing.

Address of property: _____

Asking price: _____

Date of first viewing: _____

Date of second viewing: _____

Building work and structure

Is the property free from cracks in the rendering or brickwork? In particular, look for bricks that are cracked vertically as this is an indication of serious movement.	Yes No	☐ ☐
Is the property free from 'zig-zag' cracks around the windows and doors? Make sure cracks have not been filled recently.	Yes No	☐ ☐
Does the property have some type of damp-proofing? This could be a row of slates, mineral felt or plastic sheet – look on the third or fourth brick above the ground.	Yes No	☐ ☐
Is the damp-proof course visible all around the house and free from obstruction? Look for flower beds or garden waste that might be piled above the damp-proof course.	Yes No	☐ ☐
Are gutters and drainpipes free from blockages and cracks?	Yes No	☐ ☐
Is the inside of the property free from damp? Look for stains on walls and ceilings and use your nose.	Yes No	☐ ☐
Is the roof sound and not bowing?	Yes No	☐ ☐
Are the loft, tanks and pipes insulated?	Yes No	☐ ☐
Are flat roofs free from puddles when it rains?	Yes No	☐ ☐

Windows

Do all the windows open smoothly?	Yes No	☐ ☐
Are the window frames free from rot?	Yes No	☐ ☐
Are the window frames straight and free from bowing?	Yes No	☐ ☐
Are the windows free from condensation between the panes of double glazing?	Yes No	☐ ☐

Woodwork

Do the skirting boards and floorboards join without large gaps?	Yes No	☐ ☐
Are the floorboards solid and free from bounce and creaks when you walk on them?	Yes No	☐ ☐
Is the woodwork free from the smell of damp?	Yes No	☐ ☐

Figure 9.1 Observation checklist

Is the woodwork free from small piles of dust at the base? Try touching some to find out whether it crumbles.	Yes No	☐ ☐

Electrics

Do all the sockets and plugs have square pins? If they have round pins they will need replacing and the property will probably need complete rewiring.	Yes No	☐ ☐
Are sockets placed above skirting boards? If they are on the skirting boards they will have to be moved.	Yes No	☐ ☐
Is there a fairly new date on the fuse board? If not it may need replacing.	Yes No	☐ ☐

Plumbing

Is there adequate water pressure? Try a tap at the top of the house to test this.	Yes No	☐ ☐
Is there adequate water pressure for the bath to fill efficiently?	Yes No	☐ ☐
Is the flush on the toilet adequate?	Yes No	☐ ☐
Are the sink, bath, toilet pan and cistern free from cracks and leaks?	Yes No	☐ ☐
Is the central heating system working well and efficiently? Ask the vendor to switch it on and ask about previous bills.	Yes No	☐ ☐
Are the radiators free from corrosion and leaks?	Yes No	☐ ☐

Garden and boundaries

Are all garden boundaries (fences, walls, gates or hedges) sound and intact?	Yes No	☐ ☐
Is the property secure from intrusion?	Yes No	☐ ☐
Is the garden free from unexplained wet patches or subsidence?	Yes No	☐ ☐
Are garden paths and patios free from cracks and evidence of subsidence?	Yes No	☐ ☐

Surrounding properties and neighbours

Are the areas visible from the property free from 'eyesores'?	Yes No	☐ ☐
Is the area free from obtrusive development or building work?	Yes No	☐ ☐
Are the neighbouring properties free from evidence of activities that could be annoying or disturbing?	Yes No	☐ ☐

Figure 9.1   *continued*

Investment potential

Will the property be easy to sell?	Yes	☐
	No	☐
Does the property have good letting potential?	Yes	☐
	No	☐
Is the area free from potential development which could have a negative influence on house prices?	Yes	☐
	No	☐
Is the asking price reasonable for the property type and location?	Yes	☐
	No	☐
Are property prices still rising in the area?	Yes	☐
	No	☐

Development potential

Is the property free from listed building status?	Yes	☐
	No	☐
Does the vendor have any recent planning applications that have been granted?	Yes	☐
	No	☐
Does the vendor know of any neighbouring planning applications that have been granted?	Yes	☐
	No	☐
Is there evidence of recent renovation, refurbishment or conversion of neighbouring properties? This suggests two things: planning permission may be easier to obtain and the area is becoming more popular.	Yes	☐
	No	☐
Does the property appear to be free from potential boundary disputes?	Yes	☐
	No	☐
In your opinion, is there potential for development?	Yes	☐
	No	☐

Figure 9.1 _continued_

Spotting potential for development

Spotting the potential for development is an area with which first-time developers often struggle. It is easy to get carried away with a project, thinking about all the positive aspects and turning a blind eye to the negative aspects. But, if you don't want your project to fail, you must be realistic and think about all the potential problems before you begin. Consider the following points when thinking about the potential for development:

■ Would the proposed development improve the selling/letting potential?

■ How much is the property worth now? How much could it be worth after development? Would your property be negatively affected by falling house prices?

■ Is the proposed market available once the development has been completed?

■ Is there evidence of similar development in the area?

■ What is the standard of neighbouring properties?

■ Are all the neighbouring properties well maintained?

■ Are there new cars and smart people in evidence?

■ Are there new bars and restaurants opening in the area?

■ Are there new estate agents opening in the area?

■ Is there evidence of the local authority upgrading local facilities and amenities?

There are certain projects that you should consider avoiding, as the potential for trouble is great. Why make the project much harder than it should be when there are plenty of other opportunities available? Examples of properties that you should consider avoiding are:

■ Listed buildings (it is a criminal offence to carry out works to a listed building without prior consent, and there is no guarantee that consent will be given).

■ Properties with existing boundary disputes.

■ Properties with problem neighbours (they may object to your planning application and can make your life difficult in many other ways).

■ Properties with shared/disputed access.

■ Properties in areas prone to flooding or with flooding potential (this also applies to acquiring land on river flood plains).

■ Properties located in areas with active local campaigners against development.

▌ Buildings with sitting tenants.

▌ Properties in conservation areas – you will need to apply for conservation area consent and there is no guarantee that it will be granted.

▌ Properties located in a green belt – development will be limited, restricted or denied.

▌ Properties in an area of outstanding natural beauty – development will be limited, restricted or denied.

▌ Properties underneath a flight path – potential purchasers or tenants will not like this.

▌ Properties near a planned highway development – the extra noise and pollution could put off potential purchasers or tenants. You could even lose your property under a Compulsory Purchase Order. Visit www.highways.gov.uk for information about proposed highway development.

Summary

When you view a property it is important to keep a record of your visit. This will include details of the property, your personal observations, your viewing checklist, estate agent's information, surveyor's reports and details of any previous planning applications. If you file this information carefully you will find it easier to compare and contrast properties when you make your final decision about which property to buy.

Once you have found a property in which you are interested, it is vital that you check out the neighbourhood, as there could be a number of potential problems that could ruin your plans for development. Techniques for researching the neighbourhood are discussed in the next chapter.

10 Researching the neighbourhood

Once you have found a property in which you are interested, you will need to find out more about the local neighbourhood. This is in addition to the location research you have already conducted (see Chapter 7). Neighbourhood research is specific to the location of the property in which you are interested, and involves a careful analysis of all the factors that will influence the development and investment potential of the property.

It involves an objective analysis of neighbourhood statistics and a subjective analysis of the immediate neighbourhood to find out whether there is anything that would be off-putting to potential tenants and/or buyers. This involves personal observation and questioning neighbours. Advice on how to effectively and efficiently research the neighbourhood is offered in this chapter.

Using government statistics

The Office for National Statistics (ONS) is responsible for producing a wide range of economic and social statistics. At www.neighbourhood.statistics.gov.uk you can access statistical data about the neighbourhood in which your property is located. By entering the postcode of the property you can obtain a neighbourhood profile which includes the following information:

■ details about the resident population, including information on change and density, ethnicity, gender, marital status and religion.

■ health and care information, including details of disability benefits, fertility and mortality rates;

■ signs of deprivation, including income, employment, education and health;

■ economic activity, including employment and unemployment rates;

■ land management, regeneration and economic planning;

■ education, training and skill levels of the local population;

■ housing and households, including property prices, local authority rents and tenure.

You can also access regional data on www.statistics.gov.uk. This includes regional data on the population, economy, labour market, education and training, transport, the environment and living in the region you have selected.

Statistics produced by the ONS must reach certain standards in terms of methodology and methods, and they must be politically independent and transparently produced. This means that you can access reliable, valid and unbiased information about the area in which you are interested. This information will add to the more subjective information about the neighbourhood gathered from some of the sources discussed below.

Researching environmental issues

The Environment Agency has a website which enables you to search for information about the area in which the property is located. This is useful as it will alert you to potential problems such as flooding and pollution. You can also find information on waste management, landfill sites and local water treatment sites. Although the risk may not be great, you must always think about the resale value of your property and be aware of any problems that may deter potential buyers. Consult www.environment-agency.gov.uk for more information. To use the service you will need to know the postcode or location of the property in which you are interested.

Mobile phone masts can be a deterrent for potential purchasers. You can find out the location of mobile phone masts by visiting www.sitefinder.ofcom.org.uk. This site is operated by Ofcom on behalf of central government, and includes information on all cellular radio transmitters in England, Scotland, Wales and Northern Ireland. Only operational sites are included in the database.

Questioning the neighbours

Some people are happy to discuss the neighbourhood and their experiences of living in the vicinity, whereas other people are uncomfortable talking about these issues to strangers. The only way you can find out whether someone is willing to talk to you is to introduce yourself and initiate a discussion. You will soon know whether someone is willing to talk . If people are not, thank them and leave – no one should ever be bullied or cajoled into offering an opinion. You may find the following tips helpful when approaching neighbours:

▮ Use a 'gatekeeper'. This is someone who knows people within the neighbourhood and is willing to introduce you to them. People are more willing to talk to someone who is personally introduced by someone they know and trust.

▮ Use a 'snowballing' technique. This is a technique used by researchers, who ask one person to recommend another and so on. Often people are more willing to talk to you if they know you have already had a chat with someone they know.

▮ Be honest about who you are and what you are doing.

▮ If knocking on front doors, do so at a reasonable time of day. Carry the estate agent details of the property and make sure these are in full view if knocking on neighbours' doors. This will help to show that you are thinking about buying the property and may provide a starting point for the discussion.

▮ Try to establish rapport by talking about something that will be of interest to them. Hopefully this will involve the neighbourhood.

▮ Go to places where neighbours congregate, such as the local pub, village hall or corner shop. Often pub landlords or shop owners can be a useful source of information, especially for subjective information about how an area is changing.

▪ Don't ask judgemental questions that include words such as 'good' or 'bad' neighbourhood. Keep your wording neutral.

▪ Ask open rather than closed questions. These are questions that require the respondent to answer with more than one word.

You must remember that any information you obtain from neighbours is subjective. This does not mean that it is not useful information: people are highly subjective when it comes to buying a property, and you must always have in mind the resale value of a property. If a neighbour thinks there is a problem with a neighbouring estate, so too could a potential buyer. Listen to the comments of neighbours and back up what you have heard with your own observations and with reliable statistical data.

Observing the neighbourhood

Take note of the information in Chapter 7: this provides useful advice about recognizing suitable locations. In addition to this advice there are more specific issues you should be looking for when you think you have found the right property. These involve a careful observation of what is happening in the neighbourhood.

Participant observation is a technique used by social researchers. They immerse themselves in the culture that they are observing in the hope that they will gain a deeper insight into what is going on. This is a useful technique for property developers who are intending to buy more than one property in an area. By immersing yourself in the neighbourhood you can get to know much more about what is happening. You will find out about local campaigns: schools opening or closing, mobile phone masts being erected, relief roads receiving approval. You will get to know the areas that are less popular with locals and the areas that are attracting outside buyers.

Through using this technique you will come across a 'gatekeeper' who will be able to offer you valuable information and introduce you to other people in the community. You will also be able to find out what people think about the local housing supply and the amount of private rented accommodation in the area. This is useful if you are intending to let your property. Also, make contact with local landlords, who will be able to offer information and advice about letting in the area.

When viewing the neighbourhood, take note of the following:

▮ The property boundaries: consider access, right of way, the state of adjoining properties and gardens. Look for sections of the boundary that may pose a risk to security or may be a magnet for graffiti or vandalism. This is important if you are intending to spend a long time renovating a property, as empty properties attract vandals and fly-tipping.

▮ The standard of roads and pavements, the level of street lighting, speed limits, traffic-calming measures, residential parking schemes. If a parking scheme is in place, speak to local residents about the cost, how well it works and what people think about the scheme.

▮ The amount and type of derelict land and empty properties in the vicinity. Could they attract vermin, gangs of youths, drug addicts, squatters or drunkards, all of which will put off potential buyers?

▮ The availability, type and standard of local schools, youth clubs, social facilities, health services and leisure and enter-tainment facilities. Think about your target market and make sure the facilities match this market.

▮ Look for signs of local community involvement, such as neigh-bourhood watch schemes and local campaigns. If you are intending to aim your property at the family market, this type of community structure can be appealing and a good selling point.

▮ Look for evidence of environmental campaigns and greener ways of living in the neighbourhood. What local authority waste and recycling schemes are available? Are local organiza-tions, schools and community groups getting involved in environmental projects? Are there local suppliers of envi-ronmentally friendly products, materials and services? Is there a local organic vegetable box scheme available? This type of living is becoming increasingly popular and could help to attract potential tenants and purchasers to your property.

Summary

Once you have found a property in which you are interested, you need to carry out some neighbourhood research to find out whether it is the type of place in which potential tenants/buyers would like to live. This involves an analysis of neighbourhood statistics, personal observation and discussions with people who live in the area.

If you are happy with the results of your neighbourhood research you can think about the next step of your project: buying the property. The steps involved in this process are discussed in the next chapter.

Buying a property

Once you believe you have found the right property in the right location, you need to find out whether it is being offered for the right price. If it is, you can begin the buying process.

When buying a property you need to research local prices to find out whether you are obtaining a good deal. This involves a consideration of past, present and future prices in the vicinity and an understanding of the costs involved. You also need to be able to negotiate and bargain, knowing when to make an offer and when to walk away. This is the case whether buying privately, through an estate agent or at auction. This chapter offers advice about these issues.

Knowing whether the price is right

How do you know that the property you have found represents good value for money? If you know the area well and have been keeping abreast of fluctuations in the local market, you will have a good idea about general house prices in the area. Also, if you have taken notice of the advice offered in Chapter 6, you will have conducted an effective price analysis that enables you to get a feel for when a price is right.

In addition to this research find out about the prices of properties similar to that in which you are interested. Look at similar properties in different states of repair in the vicinity. What is the selling price when they are 'in need of modernization'? What is the selling price when they have been renovated and modernized? The best way to obtain this information is to contact local estate agents and view some properties in different states of repair. Leave your details with several local estate agents and ask them to contact you as soon as this type of property appears on the market.

Visit each property and take notes. This will help you to plan your own development when you have bought the property. Note the asking price and find out how long the property has been on the market. How quickly does the estate agent expect it to sell? How quickly are similar properties selling? Keep an eye on the different properties, and when they are sold attempt to find out for how much, although some estate agents will be reluctant to offer this information.

Consult some of the websites mentioned in Chapter 6 to find out how prices have changed over the past few years. This will help you to predict how they might change in the future. Currently house prices are falling in many areas, so it is important to monitor these changes in price so that you know when to make an offer. Also, many property owners are becoming jittery about the property market and may be willing to accept a much lower offer on a property if you can prove that you can move quickly on the sale. This is also the case for properties that have been repossessed – lenders want to dispose of the property quickly and, although they are under a duty of care to obtain the best possible price, they also need to move quickly to recoup their loan. If you are able to build up a trusting relationship with local estate agents you can convince them to let you know about repossessions and other bargain properties as soon as they appear on the market, which will help you to beat the competition from other buyers and developers.

Negotiating and bargaining

Successful property developers know how to negotiate and bargain. They will very rarely offer the asking price and will be prepared to move on to another property if the vendor is unwilling to negotiate. Make sure that you do not become so attached to a property that you must have it at all costs. This does not make financial sense and is not good for your property business. If the price is not right, move on to another property.

Once you have found a property in which you are interested, decide on the lowest amount you want to offer and the highest price you are willing to pay. Do not be tempted or persuaded to raise your highest level. This is particularly important when buying at auction (see below).

When you negotiate on the price, point out the benefits the vendor would gain by dealing with you instead of someone else. If you are a cash buyer, say so. Most people are happier to deal with a cash buyer as there is no chain involved and the process can move much quicker. If you are a first-time buyer or have a prearranged mortgage, use this as a bargaining tool.

If a vendor is unwilling to negotiate on the purchase price, think about whether there are other areas on which you could negotiate. For example, you could find out whether specific items of furniture would be included in the sale. Some vendors are willing to agree to this as it reduces their own removal and/or storage costs, and this could be useful to you if you intend to let the property.

Other useful bargaining tools are the survey and/or Home Condition Report. All vendors in England and Wales are required to produce a home information pack and, although Home Condition Reports are not a required part of the pack, the government believes they are important to buyers and sellers and hopes to encourage their take up (see Chapter 21). At this present time it is unclear how many people will decide to include a Home Condition Report in their pack. If there is not one included for the house you are buying, or you are not happy with the report that is included, you should arrange to have a private survey undertaken (see below). This will alert you to any potential problems and you may be able to return to the vendor with the results of the survey and negotiate a reduced price based on these results.

Making an offer

If the property is being sold through an estate agent, you will need to make your offer through the agent. Estate agents act for vendors and earn commission on the selling price, which means they will want to get as high a price as possible. If your offer is lower than the asking price, make sure that it is still put to the vendor. Some estate agents will try to tell you that an offer below the asking price will not be accepted when this is not the case.

Verbal offers are not legally binding and you are able to pull out at any stage. If you make a written offer, make sure that you include 'subject to contract' as you can still pull out at any stage before contracts are exchanged. This is useful for some developers who find that, once the survey has been completed, the problems are too great and the property does not represent a good investment. However, you should try to act ethically. You will be in a position to sell at some point and will not want others to treat you badly.

Buying a repossession

If the property that you are interested in is a repossession the buying process can be a little different. Once you have made an offer on the property, the selling agent may decide to advertise your offer online or in the local newspaper and invite higher bids. Some will choose to use a sealed bid approach whereby all offers are invited up until the specified deadline, at which time the sealed bids are opened and the property goes to the highest bidder. Others will invite further bids right up until the time that contracts are exchanged. This can be done even when your offer has been accepted and you have begun the conveyancing process. If someone offers a higher bid the selling agent will return to you and ask whether you wish to increase your offer and if you don't you could lose the property and any legal and surveyor's fees that you have already paid. Therefore, you can reduce the chances of losing the property by moving as quickly as possible on the sale.

Alternatively, you might find it preferable to buy repossessions through auction as exchange of contracts takes place when you have made the highest bid. This means that you cannot lose the property to another bidder at a later stage (see below). More information about buying properties that have been repossessed is available in *The Complete Guide to Buying Repossessed Property* (see Chapter 1).

Arranging a survey

Once your offer has been accepted it may be prudent to arrange an independent survey, especially if the Home Condition Report is not included in the vendor's home information pack, or if you feel the existing report is not comprehensive and detailed enough for your requirements. The type of survey will depend on the age and condition of the property. All mortgage companies will carry out their own valuation survey, and some will carry out a valuation and condition survey. You can rely on these surveys if you wish, but if the property is old, derelict, empty or run-down you should always obtain a full structural survey. If buying at auction you will need to arrange the survey before you bid for the property (see below).

The results of the survey will provide you with further bargaining power concerning the price of the property. Obtain quotations for any work that would need to be carried out as recommended by the surveyor, and discuss these with the vendor.

When choosing a surveyor, obtain quotations from at least three different companies and/or individual surveyors. Ask whether they are insured and find out what is covered by this insurance. Make sure that they are fully qualified and members of the Royal Institute of Chartered Surveyors (RICS). Members have to offer independent and impartial advice, update and enhance their skills and adhere to a strict code of conduct. You are also protected by a formal complaints handling procedure. For more information about carrying out a survey and finding a qualified surveyor contact the RICS (details below).

Choosing a conveyancer

Conveyancing covers all the legal work involved in property purchase. You can choose to use a solicitor, a licensed conveyancer or do the work yourself. The last option should only be chosen by experienced developers who know what they are doing, as some of the paperwork and legal aspects can be complex.

Most firms of solicitors offer a conveyancing service, but it is advisable to choose someone who is experienced in this type of work. If you choose a conveyancer, make sure he or she is licensed. A licensed conveyancer is a specialist in property law, trained and qualified in all aspects of the law dealing with property. More information can be obtained from the Council for Licensed Conveyancers (details below).

Before choosing someone to carry out the conveyancing, obtain several quotations from different people. Check whether the figure quoted is a fixed fee or depends on how much work is involved. Also, find out whether the quotation includes the following:

- Stamp Duty Land Tax;
- search fees (these may not be necessary as they should be included in the home information pack);
- land registration fees;
- expenses;
- VAT.

Find out how much will be payable if the sale should fall through before contracts are exchanged. This is important as vendors may pull out of the sale, especially if they are involved in a long chain that breaks down.

Obtaining important documents

Before your purchase is completed you will need to obtain all the necessary paperwork and check that it is complete and correct. If you have employed the services of a solicitor or conveyancer, he or she will do this for you. This information should be included in the home information pack.

Title deeds

The title deeds should contain a series of documents detailing all the legal transactions that affect the property. There should be at least one 'deed of conveyance', also known as an 'Indenture of Conveyance' or 'transfer deed'. This shows when the land was first sold, and additional such deeds should be included for every time the land has since been sold.

A 'deed of grant' may be included with the documents if a right of way has been granted since the land was originally sold, or if utility companies have been granted permission to run their services across the land.

Other documents that might be included within the title deeds are copies of planning permissions, copies of sellers' property information forms, searches and enquiry forms.

The title deeds to land are normally held by your mortgage company as security until you repay the loan. If you make a cash purchase you will hold the deeds yourself and should have them stored in a safe place. When you come to sell you will need to include them in your home information pack.

Restrictive covenants

Restrictive covenants are an obligation that may be imposed on the owner of a property in the deeds to that property. They are most likely to be found on leasehold properties, and will include such actions as running a business from the property, carrying out building work or fixing satellite dishes to the outside walls.

However, they also may be included on freehold properties. This can be common in new housing estates where the developer has placed restrictions on building work such as extensions and conservatories to prevent unsympathetic or inappropriate development. Find out whether there are any such covenants on the property you are thinking of purchasing, as this may affect what you can do to the property and will have implications for your proposed development.

Covenants are included with the title deeds to a property, and if you are using a solicitor, you should be warned about these covenants before you make your purchase. If they are too restrictive and will affect your development plans, you may have to think about pulling out of the purchase. In some cases the covenant will require that you seek permission before carrying out alterations. Find out whether this permission is likely to be granted before making purchasing decisions.

Buying at auction

It is possible to save up to 40 per cent on the purchase price of a property by buying at auction. Given the current market conditions, more and more repossessions are appearing at auction. Many of these properties are auctioned because they are in a poor state of repair and some have been stripped of fixtures and fittings. This can be off-putting for the ordinary buyer, but useful for property developers as they can be obtained cheaply and provide a blank canvas for development projects.

However, it is also possible to make big mistakes and be lumbered with a property that is not a viable investment. To avoid these mistakes you must think carefully about buying at auction, and if you decide to follow this route you need to undertake careful and thorough research and make sure that you are not affected by 'auction fever'. This is where bidders get carried away and bid more than they wanted to pay, or more than they can actually afford.

If you intend to buy at auction, you should take note of the following points:

- Think about how much you can afford and arrange finances before the auction takes place. If your bid is successful you will have to put down a 10 per cent cash deposit on the day, and you will usually have to complete the purchase within 28 days. Often this is not enough time to arrange a mortgage, so this will have to be sorted out before you make your purchase.

- View the property. Auction houses arrange open days, and these will be detailed in the salesroom catalogue.

- Consult the home information pack to check that the title deeds, type of ownership, covenants and other paperwork are in order and that the property is suitable for your development plans. Consult the Home Condition Report if it is included in the pack. If not, arrange your own independent survey to be carried out; this will have to take place before the auction.

- Consult a builder about the costs of renovating the property before the auction.

- Your solicitor or conveyancer may need to examine the legal documents prior to the auction, and you will have to pay for these services, regardless of whether you are successful in buying the property.

■ Find out whether there are any restrictions on development, either because of the area in which the property is located or as a result of restrictive covenants in the deeds of the property.

■ Always set a price limit and don't go over this limit at the auction.

■ Try to view the whole room during bidding so that you can watch for phantom bids and check that the vendor is not bidding to raise the price on the property.

Once the gavel comes down and you are the highest bidder, it immediately becomes a binding contract and you cannot change your mind. Once you have bought at auction you cannot pull out or renegotiate a price if you find that there are major defects. On the plus side the property is yours and there is no chance of being gazumped. Also, buying a property at auction is a very quick process, and this can be useful for people who wish to begin their development project quickly.

To find out about property auctions contact local estate agents or search the various 'property auction databases' on the internet, although there is a fee for using these services.

Summary

If you are interested in buying a property, you need to check that it is being offered at the right price. You should always negotiate with the vendor to obtain the best price, and if the vendor is not willing to negotiate you should consider looking at other properties. All successful property developers are good at negotiating and know how to obtain a bargain. Once you have made an offer, you may need to arrange for a survey and for someone to carry out the conveyancing. If buying at auction, you may need to arrange a survey and solicitor before the auction takes place.

Now that you have bought the right property, in the right place, at the right price and at the right time, you can begin your development project. The first action you need to take is to obtain all the required planning permission. These issues are discussed in the following chapter.

Useful addresses

Royal Institution of Chartered Surveyors
RICS Contact Centre, Surveyor Court
Westwood Way
Coventry CV4 8JE
Tel: (0870) 333 1600
Fax: (020) 7334 3811
e-mail: contactrics@rics.org
www.rics.org
The Royal Institution of Chartered Surveyors (RICS) is the largest organization for professionals working in property, land and construction worldwide. You can find a chartered surveyor in your area by using the online search facility.

Council for Licensed Conveyancers
16 Glebe Road
Chelmsford
Essex CM1 1QG
Tel: (01245) 349599
Fax: (01245) 341300
e-mail: use enquiry form on website
www.conveyancer.co.uk
The Council for Licensed Conveyancers is the regulatory body for licensed conveyancers who are qualified specialists in property law. You can obtain the contact details of a conveyancer in your area by using the online directory.

Stage Four
Permission

12 Obtaining planning permission

If you intend to carry out building work or change the use of your land or building, you must find out whether you need to obtain planning permission. You may be forced to put right or remove any work undertaken without the necessary permission. This is costly, time-consuming and stressful. Planning law defines development as: 'The carrying out of building, engineering, mining or other operation in, on, over or under land, or the making of any material change in the use of any building or other land.'

If you are intending to carry out any work under this definition, you must seek advice about whether planning permission is required. This chapter shows you how to distinguish between the different types of planning application, illustrates how to submit an application and advises on what to do in cases of refusal.

Knowing what needs planning permission

The following list provides examples of cases where you will need planning permission. However, it is possible to provide general advice and guidance only. Individual circumstances vary, so if in doubt speak to the planning services department of your local council.

Extensions

These will need planning permission in the following circumstances:

■   if the extension would be closer to a highway then any part of your original house (unless there would be at least 20 metres between the highway and your extension);

■   if the extension would be greater than half the area of land around the original house;

■   if the extension would be higher than the highest part of the roof of the original house;

■   if the extension would be more than 4 metres high and within 2 metres of the boundary of your property;

■   if the house is terraced and the extension would increase the volume by 10 per cent or 50 cubic metres, whichever is the greater (a volume calculator is available from the Planning Portal – details below);

■   if the property is any other type of house and the volume would be increased by 15 per cent or 70 cubic metres, whichever is the greater;

■   if the extension would be to any roof slope that faces a highway;

■   if the extension would increase the height of the existing roof.

Buildings or structures in the garden

These will need planning permission in the following circumstances:

■   if the structure would be closer to a highway than any part of the original house (unless there would be at least 20 metres between the highway and the extension);

■   if over half the area of land around the original house would be covered by the structure;

■   if the height of the roof is more than 3 metres, or 4 metres if ridged.

Fuel storage tanks

These will need planning permission in the following circumstances:

- if the storage tank is for domestic heating oil and has a height of more than 3 metres above ground level or has a capacity of more than 3,500 litres;

- if the storage tank would be closer to a highway than any part of the original house (unless there would be at least 20 metres between the highway and the extension);

- if the tank is to store liquefied petroleum gas or any liquid fuel other than oil.

Porches

These will require planning permission in the following circumstances:

- if they would have a ground area greater than 3 square metres;

- if they would be higher than 3 metres above ground level;

- if they would be less than 2 metres away from a dwelling with a highway.

Gates, walls or fences

These will require planning permission in the following circumstances:

- if the property is listed;

- if they would be more than 1 metre high and next to a highway used for vehicles;

- if they would be more than 2 metres high.

Driveways and hard standings

These might require planning permission in the following circumstances:

■   if significant banking or terracing would be required;

■   if the hard standing would be used for commercial purposes such as storing goods in connection with a business or parking a commercial vehicle;

■   if a new driveway would cross a pavement or verge;

■   if you want to widen or create a driveway onto a trunk or other classified road.

Satellite dishes, aerials and antennae

In some areas you will need permission to install a satellite dish, aerials or antennae. To find out if this is the case in your area, use the satellite dish and antennae locators at: www.planningportal.gov.uk.

Special circumstances

If your property is a listed building or is located in a conservation area, national park or designated area of outstanding natural beauty, you will need to seek advice before carrying out any alterations, repairs or development.

If your planned development is not covered in the above list you can find more information at www.planningportal.gov.uk. On this site you can find useful volume and fee calculators, along with a householder's guide to development and a 'visual walkthrough' of online application procedures.

Obtaining outline consent

When you begin to plan your property development, it is advisable to find out whether you have a chance of your plans being approved. One way to do this without spending a great deal of money drawing up intricate plans is to put in an application for 'outline consent'. This is a form of planning consent designed to test the principle of whether or not a development is acceptable. It is suitable for redevelopment schemes, such as a single house dwelling right up to a multiple block of flats, on both brownfield and greenfield sites.

However, there are certain circumstances in which you cannot apply for outline consent. As a general rule, these include the developments listed below:

▌ when the proposed development is on a listed building;

▌ when you are applying for 'change of use' such as the conversion of a family home into self-contained flats;

▌ domestic extensions;

▌ commercial extensions.

When you submit an application for outline consent, the planning authority can request as much information as it requires in order to make an informed decision. In most cases you will need to include information about issues such as the number of proposed units, car parking and site density. Decisions about materials, style, design and landscaping will not have to be made at this point. Once outline consent has been given, you have three years in which to lodge a full application.

If you are hoping to buy land on which you intend to a build a dwelling, in most cases it will be offered with outline consent. Although it is possible to buy land without outline consent for a fraction of the cost, there might be strings attached and you have no guarantee that planning permission will be granted.

If you are in any doubt as to whether you are able to apply for outline consent, contact the planning services department at your local council.

Looking into change of use

If your development involves a 'change of use' of your property, you will require planning permission. This may involve the conversion of a property into flats, or could involve a change of class in the Business Use Classes such as A1 (retail), A2 (food and drink) and A3 (financial and professional services). For some changes of business use the planning authorities will require a fairly simple application. However, if you include details about the community and council benefits to be gained by making the change, you will increase your chances of success.

Other changes of business use, such as a change to A2 (food and drink) will require more detailed plans, such as information about proposed extractor ducts and alterations to shopfronts.

Finding out about permitted development

Some domestic extensions and minor alterations to your home do not require planning permission and instead can be built under 'permitted development'. However, rules and regulations are complex and before undertaking any significant building work you must find out whether you will need to obtain planning permission. Contact the planning services department at your local council for more information and advice.

Even if you do not require planning permission, most extensions and many alterations require Building Regulations approval (see Chapter 13).

In some areas of the country and on certain properties, permitted development rights are more controlled, so it is advisable to seek advice before carrying out any development work.

Preparing and submitting planning applications

If you think you may need planning permission for your property development, the steps below outline the process you should follow:

1. Contact the planning services department at your local council. Tell staff what you intend to do and seek their advice.
2. If you are advised to make an application, ask for an application form and guidelines. Find out how many forms you will need to complete and ask how much it will cost (a fee calculator is available through the 'planning portal').

3. Find out whether there are any anticipated problems. Staff will be happy to offer advice at this early stage. If there are problems, discuss possible ways of overcoming them and make sure you include these in your application.
4. Decide whether you need to make a full application or whether it would be more sensible and appropriate to make an outline application. Again, staff will be able to advise you on the best course of action.
5. If you decide to make a full application, find out what drawings and additional information will be required. At this stage you need to decide which, if any, professionals you are going to employ to help you draw up, and submit, your plans (see below).
6. Complete and return your form with the appropriate fee, drawings and additional information.

You can also make your planning application online through the 'planning portal'. This portal enables you to create a planning application and send it electronically, with attachments, to your local planning authority, if it offers this facility. Alternatively, you can print the forms and send them through the post. For more information visit: www.planningportal.gov.uk.

Using building surveyors

If you are new to property development and preparing a planning application, you may find it useful to enlist the help of an experienced building surveyor. He or she will work with you to find out exactly what you want, and discuss whether it will be both possible and permissible. A surveyor will help you to maximize the potential of your site and advise on issues such as 'affordable housing' requirements. They can offer advice on details such as landscaping, amenity space, dustbin enclosures, fire-resisting components, compartmental walls and floors, soundproofing and heat conservation. Building surveyors can also help with the preparation of plans suitable for Building Regulations purposes (see Chapter 13).

Fees vary enormously between individuals and firms. You should obtain quotations from several different companies, or employ someone through a personal recommendation. As a general guide, you might expect to pay the fees outlined below.

Survey drawings – preparation of measured survey   £200–£400
(per 50 square metres)
Planning application drawings for flat conversion (per flat)

	£450–£550
Change of use applications	£900–£1,000
Outline planning applications for:	
Single dwelling house	£2,000–£3,000
Multiple dwelling house	£2,300–£5,000
Flats development	£2,400–£4,000
Preparation and submission of planning application for:	
Single-storey extension	£800–£1,200
Loft conversion	£1,200–£1,500
Two-storey extension	£1,200–£1,500
Excavation to form basement	£1,300–£1,600

To find a chartered building surveyor in your area, contact the Royal Institute of Chartered Surveyors (RICS). It will help you to determine whether a chartered surveyor is the type of professional you need for the job, and will also offer advice on the type of surveyor needed. The RICS can be contacted through its call centre on 0870 333 1600, via e-mail: contactrics@rics.org; or more information can be obtained from its website: www.rics.org.

Making appeals in cases of refusal

You have the right to appeal against all planning refusals and against all enforcement action taken by councils. To do this you need to put together all the facts into a written statement that is then sent to the Planning Inspectorate in Bristol. An inspector is appointed to read through all submissions, visit the site and decide whether the council should have approved the application. The process may take up to four months, depending on the method of determination, which could be by writing, hearing or inquiry. Appeals in England must be submitted within three months of the refusal.

The following types of appeal are available:

■ access appeals (Countryside and Rights of Way Act 2000);

■ advertisement appeals;

■ enforcement appeals ('enforcement' refers to the council's decision to request that you put right works carried out without the necessary permission – you can appeal against this enforcement notice);

■ environmental appeals;

■ land compensation appeals;

■ lawful development certificate appeals (a lawful development certificate (LDC) is a document confirming that the use, operation or activity named in it is lawful for planning control purposes. You must apply to your local planning authority for this certificate and if they refuse your application you can appeal);

■ planning appeals.

If you are interested in making an appeal, the Planning Inspectorate provides a variety of useful leaflets that explain the process in detail. They can be downloaded from its website: www.planning-inspectorate.gov.uk. You should note, however, that there has been a huge increase in the number of appeals over the last few years and the Planning Inspectorate requests that you use the appeals procedure only as a last resort.

Summary

Before you undertake any building work on your property you must find out whether you need planning permission. If you carry out work without the required permission, you may be forced to put right or remove the works, which can be costly, time-consuming and stressful. For redevelopment schemes and new build you are advised to seek outline consent, as this will help you to find out whether you are likely to receive full planning permission in the future.

Even if you do not need planning permission for your development, you will need to make sure that all work you carry out complies with the Building Regulations Act 1991. Important features of this Act and guidance on seeking Building Regulations approval are discussed in the next chapter.

Useful addresses

National Planning Aid Unit
Unit 419, The Custard Factory
Gibb Street
Birmingham B9 4AA
Tel: 0121 693 1201
e-mail: info@planningaid.rtpi.org.uk
www.planningaid.rtpi.org.uk
Planning Aid provides 'free, independent and professional advice and support of planning issues to people and communities who cannot afford to hire a planning consultant'. In most UK regions Planning Aid is run by the Royal Town Planning Institute, which is a registered charity. Through the website you can find out whether you qualify for Planning Aid assistance and you can contact Planning Aid in your area.

13 Obtaining Building Regulations approval

Before you begin any work on a new, existing or empty property, you must find out whether you need to obtain Building Regulations approval. If you carry out work without the required approval you could face prosecution, though it is possible to make a submission after the event (see below).

As a property developer you need to understand building control, find out what type of work needs approval, know how to apply and know what to do if the required approval has not been granted. This chapter offers advice on these issues. However, Building Regulations can be complex, and if you are in doubt you should make sure that you receive the appropriate advice specific to your project before you begin work.

Understanding building control

The Building Regulations are a set of rules that have been approved by Parliament. They manage minimum standards of design and building work required for the construction of domestic, commercial and industrial buildings. They include regulations concerning the following:

- the health and safety of people in and around the building;
- energy efficiency;
- disabled access and facilities;
- fire safety;

▮ structure;

▮ drainage;

▮ ventilation.

During construction the building work is checked at various stages to make sure that it complies with Building Regulations and is in accordance with the approved plans. Written records are made during each inspection and if there are any problems they are raised with the builder and/or the applicant. Follow-up inspections are made if any remedial work is needed. If the work is completed satisfactorily a completion certificate may be issued at the end of the job if requested. This certificate will be required when you decide to sell or remortgage your property and should be included in your home information pack.

Knowing when approval is required

You will need to obtain Building Regulations approval if you intend to put up a new building, alter or extend an existing one, or provide fittings within a building such as drains or heat-producing appliances, hot-water storage, or washing and sanitary facilities. You may also require Building Regulations approval if you intend to change the use of your building, even if you are not proposing construction work.

Approval may not be required in the following circumstances:

▮ Conservatories and porches that are single storey, built at ground level, with a floor area of less than 30 square metres and with the required safety glass installed.

▮ Carports that are open on at least two sides and with a floor area of less than 30 square metres.

▮ Small detached single-storey buildings such as sheds, stores and workshops with a floor area of less than 30 square metres. These buildings must not contain sleeping accommodation, should be constructed substantially of non-combustible materials and not be within 1 metre of a boundary.

■ Detached buildings not normally used by people, such as places used to store machinery or equipment.

■ Agricultural buildings and greenhouses, as long as they are not used for retailing, exhibiting, packing or sleeping. They must be a certain distance from any building containing sleeping accommodation and must have the required fire exits.

■ Temporary buildings that will not remain on site for periods of more than 28 days.

■ Ancillary buildings only used during construction work and not containing sleeping accommodation.

Building Regulations are complex and you should obtain advice specific to your circumstances before undertaking any work. More information about what work requires approval can be obtained from your local authority or from the explanatory booklet 'Building Regulations' available from the Department for Communities and Local Government.

Making a Building Regulations application

When you apply for Building Regulations approval you can choose to use the Building Control Service of your local authority or you can use an Approved Inspector. The latter is a private sector company or practitioner that has been approved for the purpose of carrying out the Building Control Service as an alternative to your local authority. If you choose to use an Approved Inspector you must make sure that they are authorized and have the necessary insurance cover. A list of Approved Inspectors can be obtained by consulting 'The Register' on the Construction Industry Council website: www.cic.org.uk.

If you decide to use a local authority Building Control Service you can make a full plans application or a building notice application.

Full plans application

A full plans application will need to contain detailed drawings of the proposed building work; site or location plans, detailing site boundaries and the position of public sewers; fire safety drawings, where required; copies of the structural design and calculations; an application form and appropriate fee. A decision should be reached within five weeks, or, if you agree, within a maximum of two months from date of deposit. A full plans approval notice is valid for three years. If you have requested a completion certificate the local authority will issue one upon successful completion of the work. It is useful to have a completion certificate to include in your home information pack when you sell your property.

Building notice application

An alternative to a full plans application is to submit a building notice application. This will need to contain an application form, appropriate fee and, if the proposal is for a new building or extension, a site plan with boundaries, drainage and public sewers. You may also need to submit plans of the work to show that you are complying with the Regulations. This type of application does not involve the passing or rejecting of plans by the local authority, but it will come and inspect the work as it progresses to make sure that it complies with regulations. A building notice is valid for three years from the date it was submitted to the local authority.

Self-certification

In cases where the work is minor it may be possible for a competent person, such as your builder or contractor, to self-certify that their work complies with Building Regulations, as an alternative to submitting a building notice or appointing an Approved Inspector. This may be a cheaper option for you, but you must make sure that your builder qualifies as a competent person and that the work is suitable for self-certification. Seek expert advice if in doubt.

Applying for a regularization certificate

If you have carried out building work without first obtaining Building Regulations approval it is possible to apply for a regularization certificate. This is similar to making a normal full plans submission, but after the event.

To make a regularization application you need to submit an application form together with plans of the building work, plans of as-built construction, a site location plan and the appropriate fee.

Once you have submitted your application you will be visited by a building control surveyor who will need to inspect the work. This may involve digging a hole alongside foundations to check the structure, or the removal of sections of the wall or ceiling. If the work is satisfactory and complies with the regulations, you will be issued with your certificate. A regularization certificate acts in the same way as a completion certificate. However, there is no guarantee that existing work will comply with the regulations, and if it does not a certificate will not be issued.

Working with an architect

An architect can advise you on planning permission, Building Regulations, health and safety, and deal with the authorities on your behalf. If you decide to employ an architect you will need to agree on the scope and cost of architectural services before the project is started. You can decide how much of the architect's services you wish to use, from an initial design discussion through to full completion of the project. All negotiations should be agreed in writing, and you should develop a good working relationship with your architect.

Architects' fees can be based on a percentage of the total construction cost, on the amount of time taken for the project or on an agreed lump sum. When choosing an architect ask for a breakdown of the fees involved. Speak to several architects to find out what services they can offer and the prices they charge. You will also need to consider the following issues before you meet with a potential architect:

■   the aims and objectives of the project;

■   your design style: this will include decisions about sustainable/
     ecological design, compatibility with existing buildings and
     personal taste;

■   the intended use of the building after completion;

■   information about who is in charge of the work, from day-to-
     day running to decisions about the design and overall cost;

■   your expectations about the project: how long you expect it to
     last and what you hope to achieve with the final development.

For more information about choosing and working with an
architect, contact the Royal Institute of British Architects
(details below).

Summary

Building Regulations detail the minimum standards of building
work required for the construction, extension, alteration and
change of use of buildings. These standards ensure that buildings
are structurally sound, safe in the event of fire, reasonably sound-
proof and resistant to the penetration of damp and moisture. All
plans for building work are checked for compliance with these
regulations before and during construction.

When carrying out construction work you must make sure that
you obtain the necessary planning permission and Building
Regulations approval. You also need to comply with the Party
Wall Act if you are to overcome problems and avoid disputes.
These issues are covered in the next chapter.

Useful addresses

Royal Institute of British Architects
RIBA Client Services
66 Portland Place
London W1B 1AD
Tel: (020) 7580 5533
Fax: (020) 7255 1541
e-mail: info@inst.riba.org
www.riba.org
The Royal Institute of British Architects (RIBA) is a member organization with over 30,000 members worldwide. You can find an architect using one of the online directories.

Overcoming problems and avoiding disputes

As a property developer you must make sure that you comply with all the necessary Building Regulations, as discussed in the previous chapter. In addition to adhering to these regulations, you should become familiar with the Party Wall Act 1996 and understand issues surrounding boundary disputes. This should help to minimize problems with your development.

However, some problems and disputes may be unavoidable. In these cases it is vital that you have adequate insurance to cover you against damage to your property and injury to yourself and people working on your property. This chapter offers advice on these issues.

Understanding the Party Wall Act 1996

The Party Wall Act 1996 is relevant if you live in England or Wales and wish to carry out building work of the following types:

- building on an existing wall or structure shared with another property;

- constructing a free-standing wall or the wall of a building up to or astride the boundary with a neighbouring property;

- excavating within 3 metres of your neighbour's building or structure or within 6 metres if the excavations will cut a line drawn downwards at 45 degrees from the bottom of the neighbour's foundations.

The Act states that you must not cause unnecessary inconvenience, which includes the time when building works starts and finishes. You must provide temporary protection for any adjacent buildings and make good any damage caused by the building work.

Defining a party wall

A 'party wall' stands astride the boundary of land belonging to two or more different owners, and can be a part of one building, separate two or more buildings, or consist of a 'party fence wall'. The last stands astride a boundary line but is not part of a building, for example a garden wall. A garden fence would not be included under this definition.

Service of notice

The Act states that you must give notice of your intentions to adjoining owners, even if the work will not extend beyond the centre line of the party wall. If you fail to provide notice, adjoining owners can stop the work through obtaining a court injunction. The best course of action is to keep on friendly terms with your neighbours and informally discuss your proposals with them so that the service of notice does not come as a surprise. This way they are more likely to agree to your proposals.

When you serve notice you must do so in writing and include your name and address, and the address of the property if it is different, a full description of what you propose to do and the date on which you intend to start the work. The letter needs to be dated and sent at least two months before you start work on an existing boundary. If you are intending to start work on a new wall on a boundary line or start excavations within 3 metres of your neighbour's foundations or within 6 metres of a neighbouring property (if the works will cut a line drawn downwards at 45 degrees from the bottom of the neighbour's foundation), you will need to give at least one month's notice.

The adjoining owner may respond in one of four ways: by giving consent in writing, by disagreeing in writing, by serving a counter-notice or by doing nothing.

Your neighbour should respond within 14 days of your written notice. If you do not receive a response within this time, a dispute is regarded as having arisen. Even if the neighbour intends to serve a counter-notice, he or she should let you know within the 14-day period that he or she intends to do this. The neighbour must then serve the counter-notice within a month of your notice. You must respond within 14 days to this counter-notice, otherwise a case of dispute is deemed to have arisen.

Service of notice under the Party Wall Act may not be required in the following circumstances, although if you are in doubt you should seek further advice:

- drilling into a wall to fix plugs and screws for ordinary shelving or units.

- cutting into a party wall to add or replace recessed electrical wiring or sockets.

- replastering an existing wall.

Cases of dispute

If you are unable to reach agreement with your neighbour, an 'agreed surveyor' will need to be appointed to draw up an 'award'. This is an agreement which sets out the conditions of the work, including starting dates, timing of the work, a record of the existing condition of the structure and access required. The surveyor does not need any special qualifications, but it is useful to appoint someone who is familiar with construction work and the Party Wall Act, such as a member of the Faculty of Party Wall Surveyors (details below). The applicant cannot use a surveyor who is helping with the building work, and is responsible for paying the surveyor.

The person you choose will need to be agreed by both you and your neighbour. If agreement cannot be reached, you will both need to appoint separate surveyors who will then work together to draw up an award. Under the rules of the Act they will need to work impartially and take both of your circumstances into account. If your neighbour won't appoint a second surveyor, you can appoint someone on his or her behalf.

The award is final unless you or your neighbour decide to make an appeal to the county court. This must be done within 14 days, and can only be done if one party thinks the surveyor's award is fundamentally wrong.

Gaining access

Under the Act your neighbour must provide reasonable access for your workers and/or surveyor for the purpose of carrying out the work. However, you must give your neighbour at least 14 days' notice if you wish to access his or her property. It is an offence for your neighbour to refuse access if you have followed correct procedures. Again, it is best to discuss all changes with your neighbour and point out that it is also in his or her interests to allow workers in because the work can be finished properly on both sides.

If the adjoining property is empty, you may gain access after following proper procedures and if accompanied by a police officer.

Avoiding boundary disputes

Boundary disputes are becoming more common in the United Kingdom. The most common types of boundary dispute involve high hedges, locating the true position of the boundary and obstructed right of way. The best way to avoid boundary disputes is to not buy into them in the first place. When you view properties, make sure that there are no obvious boundary problems such as high hedges and blocked rights of way, and check that the boundaries you can see are the same as are registered with the Land Registry. You can check these boundaries for a small fee. If they don't match, think again about buying the property.

Once you have bought a property, the best way to deal with any potential boundary dispute is to remain on good terms with your neighbours and attempt to discuss and resolve any problems amicably. However, if you are unable to do this, you will need to be aware of your rights and those of your neighbours before you consider taking action.

High hedges

If you think your neighbour's hedge is too high and you believe it to be restricting the use or enjoyment of your property, you are entitled to make a complaint. However, you can only do this if the hedge is evergreen – deciduous trees and hedges are not covered under current legislation. Also, you cannot complain about the height of a hedge that is jointly owned between you and your neighbour.

People do not need to seek permission to grow a hedge over 2 metres in height, and the local authority will not automatically take action if the hedge is high. It will act only if it receives a complaint, and it will judge each case individually. The local authority will take into account your situation, that of the hedge owner and the wider community. More information about high hedges can be obtained from the Department for Communities and Local Government website: www.communities.gov.uk.

Boundary location

Boundary location disputes are incredibly hard to solve, so don't buy into such a problem if at all possible. This is because the Land Registry is not responsible for defining boundaries and it is not possible for it to know the exact location of a boundary. The red edging on the Land Registry title plan is not definitive and in some cases can be misleading.

If a dispute should arise on a property you own, contact the Land Registry and obtain a copy of the register entry for your neighbour's title and compare this with your own. However, if your neighbour's land is unregistered, the Land Registry will be unable to help. You may find that the dispute cannot be resolved even by comparing title deeds. Legal definitions of boundaries are complex, and if you really want to dispute the location of a boundary you will have to obtain legal advice.

Right of way

If the dispute concerns a private right of way, such as entry into the rear of your property through a neighbour's garden, and that way has been blocked, again you may find it difficult to challenge.

In some cases the right of way may have gone completely unrecorded. Although this does not mean the right of way does not exist, it might be difficult to prove.

Again, you should avoid these problems by not buying into them. When searching for property, check front and rear entrances and see that all rights of way are clear and understood between neighbours. It is better to buy properties that do not need rights of way over other land. If you want to dispute a right of way, you will need to seek legal advice.

Obtaining insurance

One of the best ways to protect yourself, your family, your workers, your development and your finances from problems is to obtain the appropriate insurance. It is not worth trying to save money by not taking out insurance. Although you may think you will never need to claim, it is not worth taking the risk. As with all financial services, shop around for the best deal and don't be persuaded to take out more insurance than you need.

If you are intending to let your property to tenants, you must advise and obtain consent from all mortgage and insurance companies. Failure to do this may mean that insurance companies refuse to pay when you make a claim. Your property is treated as a business, and you will need to make sure that you obtain the appropriate insurance. There are specialist insurance companies that arrange insurance for landlords: details can be obtained from the Residential Landlords Association, the National Landlords Association or from your buy-to-let mortgage lender.

Buildings insurance

This insurance gives cover for buildings, and is compulsory when you take out a mortgage. However, you do not have to take out this cover with your mortgage lender, although some might charge an administration fee if you decide to use another company. Some lenders may attach this cover to their more attractive mortgages, so you should check whether this is the case when arranging your loan.

Buildings insurance should represent the full rebuilding cost of your property, not its market value. You should make sure that your property is not undervalued – you can ask a qualified surveyor to calculate a professional re-build cost or most insurance companies will provide a quotation based on the information you provide.

If you are intending to let your property to vulnerable tenants, these are classed as 'high-risk' groups and some insurers may refuse to insure your property. Some policies include the extra option of malicious damage by tenants. This is a useful option to consider, and can be well worth the extra premium.

You should also obtain insurance that covers you for loss of rent if your property remains empty as a result of damage caused by perils such as fire, explosion, smoke, impact, subsidence, maliciousness and theft.

Contents insurance

If you are intending to let your property, you can choose to take out limited contents cover which is suitable for part-furnished or unfurnished properties. You can also receive employer's liability and landlord's liability cover with your contents policy. This will provide cover against injuries, accidents or deaths to tenants or employees caused by faulty equipment, fittings or fixtures.

Fully furnished properties should have full contents cover, and you should make sure that you are not under-insured. Work out how much it costs to replace items, not their actual value.

Your tenants should be encouraged to take out their own contents insurance as this will cover them for their belongings and the items within the house for which they have responsibility.

Landlord's liability insurance

As a landlord you are responsible for the safety of the property in which your tenants live. If tenants harm themselves while in your property, they could make a claim against you. This insurance covers you for any damages that may be awarded against you and should cover all legal costs.

Employer's liability insurance

This insurance covers claims for death or injury of anyone you employ to work on your property. Some buildings insurance will include this cover in the policy, so you should check whether this is the case. If you intend to let your property to students or people on state benefits, the university and/or local authority may request that you have cover of up to £5 million.

Property owner's liability insurance

This insurance covers injury, death or damage to individuals on or adjacent to your property, such as meter readers, postal workers and council employees. This may be included in your buildings insurance, but some of the cheaper policies will not have this included, so you may need to take out extra cover.

Emergency assistance insurance

This insurance will cover you and your tenants in emergencies, and will provide a 24-hour helpline. It is useful for landlords who live away from their property, and includes emergencies such as lost keys and failure of gas, electricity and cooking facilities.

Legal expenses insurance

It is useful to have this insurance in case of disputes with tenants or workers that can only be resolved by legal and court action. Possession hearings can be expensive, and this insurance will cover solicitor, court and bailiff costs.

Rent guarantee insurance

This insurance will cover the rent on your property if tenants are unable or unwilling to pay, and will usually cover you for a set period, such as 6 or 12 months. This insurance may also cover legal expenses.

Buy-to-let insurance cover

This is a whole package of essential cover now offered to landlords to protect their investment. It should include all the cover outlined above, but you will need to check that this is the case. This cover also protects you against losing your capital investment and can help to protect the income you receive from your tenants. Obtaining comprehensive cover of this type is of particular importance during times of market uncertainty.

Life insurance

This cover guarantees a specific sum of money to a designated beneficiary upon the death of the insured. Life cover can be attached to a mortgage so that upon your death the outstanding amount on the loan will be paid. Life insurance can include a critical illness plan.

Critical illness cover

You can take out insurance to cover yourself for critical illness. On some policies you can specify for which illnesses you require cover, or pay an extra premium for complete cover. This cover pays out an agreed lump sum upon the diagnosis of a specified critical illness. You must check the small print on this cover because some illnesses will not be included, and you may not be covered if you have already received treatment for certain conditions.

Accident, sickness and unemployment insurance

This is also known as mortgage payment protection insurance. In the event of accident, sickness or involuntary unemployment, the insurance will cover your mortgage payments. Some lenders include this insurance cover with some types of mortgage, so you should check whether this is the case. You do not have to arrange this cover with your mortgage lender, so you can shop around for the best deal.

Renovation insurance

Some companies will offer a complete package of renovation insurance that includes some of the different types of insurance mentioned above. Policies vary, but you will be able to receive insurance cover for your whole renovation project, whether you intend to carry out the work yourself or employ others. This will cover you against personal injury, loss, and damage to your property or equipment.

Summary

Many problems and disputes can be overcome by not buying into them in the first place. When you view a property, make sure that you check out the boundaries and rights of way. If anything doesn't seem right, question the vendor and try to speak to the neighbours. You will soon get a feel for existing problems. Also, check that the title deeds match the boundaries you have seen. Always try to get on with your neighbours and talk to them about any proposed work so that you can reduce the possibility of disputes arising.

It is important to take out adequate insurance so that if problems do occur you are covered financially. Another way to protect yourself financially is to make sure that you organize, plan and control your finances carefully. These issues are discussed in the next chapter.

Useful addresses

Faculty of Party Wall Surveyors
19 Church Street
Godalming
Surrey GU7 1EL
Tel: 01424 883300
Fax: 01424 883300
e-mail: enq@fpws.org.uk
www.fpws.org.uk
Members of the Faculty of Party Wall Surveyors are experienced in the proper workings of the Party Wall Act 1996. They can be employed to serve the appropriate notices for you and to see that the Act is properly implemented. You can obtain advice from a professional in your area for no initial fee.

Stage Five
Perspiration

Developing and managing your budget

Planning your budget carefully is an extremely important part of your development project. So many projects fail because investors have been unrealistic about the costs involved or have not kept tight controls on the budget.

Chapter 4 offers advice about planning your finances, which will help you to think about the financial viability of your project. Now it is important to look at the specific details of the budget: how to plan carefully, understand the costs, work within the budget and control costs. This chapter offers advice on successfully developing and managing your budget.

Planning your budget

To be able to plan your budget successfully you must be aware of all the costs involved at the beginning of your project, from buying the property to decorating and furnishing. All quotations should be obtained well in advance. These include the fees of professionals, taxes, mortgage fees, building work and materials, fixtures, fittings, furniture and decoration.

Once you have worked out all the costs involved, you need to provide a contingency fund. This is available for unavoidable costs for which you have not planned. Even the most carefully planned budget may require extra funding. It is a good idea to provide around 15 per cent of your total budget as a contingency fund. That way, you will not be left short or find yourself struggling financially when unexpected expenses arise.

Knowing about the costs

Throughout your development project there will be a variety of costs for which you must budget. These can be divided into three stages. The first includes all the initial costs involved with buying a property. The second includes all the costs involved in renovating and/or refurbishing a property. The third involves day-to-day running costs.

Stage 1: buying a property

When you begin the buying process, there are a number of fees you will have to pay. These may include the following, depending on the services and organizations you intend to use.

Solicitor's fees
You can hire a solicitor to do your conveyancing. You may have to pay search fees as they occur, and these will be in the region of £70–£250, although some searches will be included in the home information pack and therefore paid for by the vendor. The rest of the bill will need to be paid around the time of completion. Fees vary, but will be in the region of £600–£1,000. Some mortgage companies offer to pay solicitor's fees as part of the mortgage deal, though you may have to use a solicitor of their choice.

Conveyancing fees
If you decide to use a licensed conveyancer rather than a solicitor, you can expect to pay around £300–£500. Property developers who are more experienced may decide to undertake the conveyancing themselves, although most mortgage companies will require a licensed conveyancer to act for them.

Surveyors' fees
A valuation survey will be undertaken by your mortgage company and should cost in the region of £170–£300. If your mortgage company decides to carry out a valuation and condition survey this should cost £250–£500. The price of a full structural survey depends on the type of survey you choose, the size and price of the

property, the company you choose and the mortgage lender you decide to use, but should be in the region of £400–£1,000. Some vendors may include a Home Condition Report in their home information pack and you will need to decide if this is adequate or whether you wish to pay for an independent survey.

Stamp Duty Land Tax (SDLT)

You do not have to pay SDLT on properties with a purchase price of less then £125,000 (residential) or £150,000 (non-residential). If the property is in a disadvantaged area, you do not have to pay SDLT on properties with a purchase price of less than £150,000.

If the purchase price of a residential property is £125,000–£250,000, you will pay 1 per cent of the purchase price (£150,000–£250,000 in disadvantaged areas). If the purchase price is £250,000–£500,000, you will pay 3 per cent of purchase price, and if the purchase price exceeds £500,000, you will pay 4 per cent SDLT.

Mortgage broker fee

If you decide to use a mortgage broker to find and arrange your mortgage, you should find out whether there is a fee for the service. Although most brokers get commission from the mortgage lender, some will charge their customers. The fee might be up to £300.

Mortgage booking fee

In most cases you will have to pay an administration fee to the mortgage lender to reserve the mortgage funds. These fees vary enormously and depend upon the company you are using, but should be in the region of £100–500. Fees tend to be higher on the more favourable mortgage deals.

Reinspection fee

Some mortgage lenders may withhold part of the loan until you carry out agreed repairs to the property. They will then need to reinspect the property before they release the money, and some companies charge for this service, usually from £50 to £300.

Deposit
When you exchange contracts on a property you will need to pay a deposit, which your solicitor handles. The amount of the deposit will depend on the purchase price, your available funds and the amount of money the mortgage company is willing to lend. In today's economic climate, the larger a deposit you can pay, the better mortgage deal you are likely to obtain.

Purchase price
Once you have agreed on the price, you may be able to negotiate a reduction, depending on the result of your survey. If expensive problems have been identified, you need to work out how much it would cost to rectify them, and find out whether the vendor is willing to negotiate. Mortgage repayments will begin in the same month that completion has occurred, so you will need to start to budget for this from the first month of ownership.

Stage 2: renovation/refurbishment costs

Labour
You will need to budget for any outside labour you intend to use. Obtain written quotations from several builders, traders or service suppliers, and make sure that your contract includes a clause to cover extra work and extra costs that may occur (see Chapter 17).

Materials
During this planning stage you need to think about all the materials you require and obtain quotations from local suppliers. This will involve researching builders' merchants, trade discount stores and other local suppliers (see Chapter 19), and you may need to budget for delivery. If you are using a builder, find out whether materials are included in the quotation.

Equipment
If you intend to carry out the work yourself you will need to budget for equipment, which includes all the tools you will require for the project. You need to think about your existing supply, tools which can be borrowed or hired, and those that you need to buy. You may also need to budget for the cost of storage

and insurance. Costs can be kept down by purchasing only what is absolutely necessary.

Plant hire
If your development is large in scale, you need to think about plant hire. This may include skips, scaffolding and cement/ concrete mixers. Check with your builder that these are included in the overall fee for building work, and find out what insurance is included.

Fixtures and fittings
This includes everything you will need to provide to make the accommodation habitable, for example lighting, kitchens, bathrooms, flooring, sockets, built-in cupboards and fireplaces. You will need to find a good local supplier who can provide the products at the right price and at the right time (see Chapter 19). Make sure you negotiate on bulk deals and make use of trade cards and discounts.

Furnishings
This will include everything you need to provide to 'dress' the house for sale or to furnish the property for tenants. You can consider second-hand furniture and fabrics if they meet current fire regulations and if they look good (see Chapter 19). Careful research is needed so that you can provide an accurate costing for your budget.

Decoration
You will need to budget for decoration, which includes paints, tiles and anything else required to make your property look good (see Chapters 20 and 21). You can save money and provide a more accurate costing by keeping to a simple colour scheme throughout the property.

Removal/storage
You may need to budget for the removal of possessions from one property to another, or for storing furniture while a property is renovated. These costs can be kept down by only buying a small amount of furniture, once a project is complete, which can then be sold with the property.

Stage 3: running costs

Mortgage repayments

The amount of repayment will depend on the size of loan, the type of mortgage and the repayment period. The mortgage still has to be paid when the property remains without tenants or unsold.

Early repayment charge

If you decide to pay off your mortgage early, you may have to pay a fee. This will depend on the agreement you sign when you take out a mortgage. Many interest-only deals enable you to pay off a certain percentage of your loan each year without charge.

Administration costs

This includes the preparation of contracts, postage, stationery and the purchase of any equipment you may need, such as computers, printers, fax machines and photocopiers. There are a variety of budgeting software packages on the market specifically designed for small businesses and property developers. These range in price from £50 to £300.

Transport

This will depend on how close you live to your property, and can be a significant cost if you live at a distance, especially as fuel prices continue to rise. If you are intending to carry out the work yourself, you need to think about how you are going to transport large materials and equipment to the site. You may need to budget for delivery charges.

Insurance

At the very least you will need to budget for buildings insurance, which can be in the region of £150–£400. You will also need to think about a variety of other types of insurance (see Chapter 14).

Cleaning

If you intend to clean the property yourself you need to budget for cleaning equipment and products. Developers with a number of properties will need to budget for the services of a cleaner or cleaning company.

Maintenance

Regular maintenance will be required for properties that you intend to let (see Chapter 25). You will have to budget for the areas of maintenance for which you have responsibility, such as cleaning gutters and replacing roof tiles.

Replacement

If items get damaged, lost or stolen, you will need to replace them. You need to set aside a part of your budget for this replacement. It is difficult to know how much you will need as this depends on your tenants and the items that are damaged. You will also need to consider the excess on your contents insurance policy. Larger excesses mean you can reduce the price of your policy, but this may be a false economy if you have to replace a number of items during the tenancy.

Management

Depending on the type of management you intend to use for your project, you may have to provide extra funding. For example, you may decide to employ a project manager to run the project (see Chapter 16), or to use a letting agency to look after your property (see Chapter 23). Obtain written quotations and shop around for the best deal, remembering that this may not necessarily be the cheapest.

Finance

Depending on the nature of your company and your personal skills and experience, you may need to employ an accountant or a bookkeeper (see Chapter 4). All professionals should provide you with a guide to their fees and you should consult several people before making your decision.

Utilities

This may include initial connection charges and any gas, electricity and water charges that you are paying while you are working on a property or waiting to sell a property. It may also include any bills that you have agreed to pay for your tenants.

Council tax

You will need to budget for council tax payments. You can find out the band of your property by contacting the local authority or by consulting www.voa.gov.uk. Your tenants will be responsible for paying the council tax when you let your property, although if it is occupied solely by students an exemption applies. If your property is considered to be 'uninhabitable' you may not be required to pay council tax for up to six months, but you will need to check this with your local authority.

Working within your budget

Your budget is important and if you are serious about your investment you must treat your budget seriously. Don't be tempted to spend more than the amount for which you have budgeted, unless it is absolutely unavoidable, in which case your contingency fund can be used.

Refer to your budget often. It will help you to make sensible decisions about sourcing materials and buying fixtures and fittings. It will also help you to be ruled by your head, rather than your heart, which is important for successful property development.

It is possible to make savings. If you find that you have underspent on one part of your budget, don't automatically think that you can overspend on another. Instead, add this saving to your contingency fund for use in emergencies. Your contingency fund should always be available and may need to be topped up on a regular basis.

Controlling costs

Beginner property developers can find that their costs quickly spiral out of control. This problem can be avoided through careful budgeting, strict personal discipline and thorough price research. It is also very important to have a well-worded, legally binding contract with any builders or traders you employ. This should include information about what will happen if the work takes longer than expected or costs more than expected. This will stop building costs getting out of control. Only use reputable builders who have been recommended by others. It is important to develop a good working relationship with people you employ. If you have problems, think about employing someone else (see Chapter 17).

Some people find that they are lacking in personal discipline and that it is very hard not to be tempted by nice furniture and expensive fixtures and fittings. If you know that you are this type of person it might be better to employ a project manager who is able to control the budget for you (see Chapter 16). If this is not financially viable you could ask a partner or friend you trust to control the budget.

Summary

All successful property developers realize the importance of careful budget development and management. This involves thorough research into the costs involved, from start-up costs to day-to-day running costs. It is also important to have a contingency fund to help pay for unavoidable expenses.

Once you have developed your budget you need to think about managing your project. Whether you undertake this task yourself or employ someone else, a good project manager will be able to develop and control your budget efficiently and effectively. These issues are covered in the next chapter.

16 Managing your project

Now that you have developed your budget you need to decide who is going to manage the development project. This role is carried out by a project manager. You may decide to appoint a separate person to undertake this task or you may decide to undertake the management yourself.

Managing a development project can be a stressful task, especially for first-time developers. It is important to appoint the right person with the right skills and expertise so that the project runs smoothly and is completed on time and to budget. This chapter offers advice on choosing a good project manager, knowing what skills are required and developing a management brief.

Appointing a project manager

The decision to appoint a project manager will depend on several factors, including the size of the job, the time, the available finance and your personal expertise.

If you are undertaking a large, expensive project and you have the finances available, you should consider appointing someone else to oversee the work. If you make the choice carefully, all the pressure is taken from you and you have an experienced, qualified person who is able to make sure that the work is completed effectively and efficiently. A good project manager will be able to carry out the following tasks:

■ prepare the project and feasibility study;

■ advise on or find sources of funding for the project;

■ offer advice about planning permission and Building Regulations and deal with the relevant authorities;

■ offer advice on health and safety issues and carry out a risk assessment;

■ arrange contracts with workers;

■ liaise with builders and traders to ensure that the work is carried out to your specification and in the correct sequence (see Chapter 17);

■ make sure the work is carried out to a good standard without defects;

■ avoid site problems, such as boundary disputes, subsoil problems, logistical errors with materials, access problems and adverse covenants;

■ manage finances and avoid common financial errors, especially with uncertain costs and unrealistic assumptions;

■ ensure that all building complies with statutory requirements;

■ achieve certainty of completion.

When appointing a project manager, find out whether he or she has professional indemnity insurance. Although some professionals shy away from this insurance because of negative perceptions about costs, it is essential for providing cover against allegations of breach of duty of care. As the client, this will offer you extra protection should legal liabilities be established against your project manager.

Depending on the size and nature of your project, you could choose a building designer, architect, quantity surveyor, building manager or a professional project manager to manage your development. When choosing this person you should make sure he or she has the necessary skills and expertise described below. Your project manager should be a member of a respected trade body or organization, such as the Chartered Institute of Architectural Technologists or the Association for Project Management (APM) (see below). Members have to update their skills regularly and adhere to a strict code of conduct, which should help to protect your interests.

Preparing a contract

Standard contract documents can be obtained through the RICS or through the APM. If the person you are considering is a member of one of these organizations, he or she will have access to these contracts free of charge. This contract should include a 'scope of services' section that details all the services you require from the project manager and the fees he or she will charge for these services.

Managing the project yourself

Smaller development projects can be self-managed as there is less work involved and less need to employ a large number of builders and tradespeople. However, although the project is smaller, you still need to make sure that you have the required skills and time to manage the project well. If you do not have the required skills, you need to think about ways to develop them before the project starts (see Chapter 3).

If you decide to manage the project yourself you should produce a management brief, as this will set out the tasks required of you and help you to think about all the issues involved in project management (see below).

It is possible to appoint project managers at different stages during the development. If you find that you are unable to continue managing your project, either because you do not have the time or skills required, or because your circumstances change, it may be preferable to appoint an outside project manager to complete the work for you. If you decide to do this you will need to produce a 'scope of services' document that lists what you require of the project manager so he or she can provide an accurate quotation for the work.

Understanding the skills and qualities required

The following skills and qualities are important for a project manager, whether you decide to appoint someone or manage the project yourself:

- well-developed leadership and communication skills;

- an ability to understand and empathize with your aims, objectives, vision and goals;

- adequate technical skills and experience;

- an understanding of the whole construction process from obtaining the necessary permission to successful completion;

- an ability to plan and think strategically;

- good delegation, negotiation and management skills;

- an ability to establish rapport and be trusted by a variety of different workers;

- an ability to coordinate and manage a diverse range of workers and an understanding of the correct sequence of trade;

- a good knowledge of risk assessment procedures and an understanding of health and safety issues;

- an understanding of when and how to seek specialist knowledge and expertise;

- an ability to fit in with the rest of the team.

This list of qualities and skills will help you to know what to look for if you decide to appoint a project manager. Find out about these during the interview stage, requesting a CV and references to follow up before making the appointment. Try to speak to previous satisfied clients.

Preparing a management brief

Whether you decide to appoint a project manager or carry out the role yourself, you will need to prepare a management brief. This is a document that sets out details of your project and the services you require from the project manager. If you are appointing an outside manager you will need to provide this list so he or she understands exactly what is required and is able to provide a full quotation for the services. The brief should include the following information:

■ introduction to the project and proposed development;

■ background, including the results of any feasibility studies carried out or required;

■ site and context, including information about adjacent properties and other development within the area;

■ programme of works, including timetable and completion date;

■ scheme management – who has overall responsibility and with whom will the project manager need to liaise?

■ responsibilities of the project manager, including budget management, procurement, contract arrangements, liaison and coordination.

Summary

Appointing a good project manager is crucial to the success of your development project. If you intend to manage the project yourself, you must be realistic about your personal skills and experience, and be willing to update these skills if necessary. It is possible to bring in an outside project manager once the work has begun if you are unable to complete the task yourself.

One of the main roles of the project manager is to appoint and oversee the work of builders, traders and service suppliers. This involves agreeing a schedule of works, sorting out contracts, making sure that work is carried out in the correct sequence and ensuring that health and safety requirements are met. These issues are discussed in the next chapter.

Useful addresses

Chartered Institute of Architectural Technologists
397 City Road
London EC1V 1NH
Tel: (020) 7278 2206
Fax: (020) 7837 3194
e-mail: use online form
www.ciat.org.uk
The Chartered Institute of Architectural Technologists (CIAT) is internationally recognized as the qualifying body for Chartered Architectural Technologists and Architectural Technicians. You can hire a member to provide your architectural design services. He or she will negotiate the construction project and manage the project from conception through to completion. You can find a member in your area by using the online directory.

Association for Project Management
150 West Wycombe Road
High Wycombe
Buckinghamshire HP12 3AE
Tel: (0845) 458 1944
Fax: (01494) 528 937
e-mail: info@apm.org.uk
www.apm.org.uk
The APM is an independent professional body for project management across Europe. Members have to be fully qualified, experienced professionals. Contact the APM for more information about choosing a project manager.

Working with subcontractors and builders

Most larger development projects will require the services of builders, traders and/or service providers. Some first-time property developers find this aspect of their project daunting, especially when they have no experience of employing workers. This feeling can be compounded by some builders who take over the project and do the work when and how they wish, rather than to the specification and timescale of the person requiring the work. Although this can work well if the builder is experienced and conscientious, it can lead to problems if this is not the case.

As the developer and investor, you must remain in charge of your project. This involves careful planning, negotiation, delegation and management. You also need to understand how to choose and employ builders, traders and service providers, and provide suitable conditions under which they can work. This chapter offers advice on these issues.

Choosing builders, traders and service providers

As a property developer you will find it very useful to draw up a list of good, reliable builders, traders and service providers. This will save you time, money and hassle, especially if they agree to be available at short notice and during emergencies. Even if you intend to do most of the repairs and renovation yourself, you will still need to employ qualified electricians and CORGI-registered plumbers if you do not have the necessary qualifications. The following steps will help you to choose good workers:

1. Start with referrals – do other property investors in your area know of good workers? Do friends, family and neighbours know of anyone they could recommend? You can also contact respected trade bodies who will be able to supply you with a list of people in your area. Don't be tempted to use traders who cold call.

2. Write down a list of the work you want completed and explain this clearly to people providing an estimate.

3. Always obtain a written estimate, even if someone has been recommended to you. Make sure there is not a call-out fee for this service. It is useful to obtain at least three estimates from different people or companies so that you can compare prices and find out whether quotations are realistic. It also gives you a chance to gain different perspectives on the type of work required. When you ask for estimates, ask also for confirmation on whether planning permission will be required and find out how long the work will take to complete.

4. Ask for references from satisfied customers and make sure you follow them up. Find out whether the person or company has carried out similar work in your area, and make arrangements to inspect the work or speak to the customer.

5. Check that the person or company is a member of a respected trade organization. Do your research – make sure the trade organization is legitimate and that membership is up to date. All respected trade organizations will be happy to help with your enquiries and most will help you to solve cases of dispute.

6. Make sure that the person or company is insured. Ask to see a public liability insurance certificate. Also, you may need to check whether the building work will affect your own building and contents insurance.

7. Find out what warranties and guarantees are included.

8. Ask about payment and deposits. It is best to agree to pay upon satisfactory completion of the work, but some companies will not agree to this if it is a long, expensive job, or if materials have

to be custom-made. In the latter cases they may require a deposit at the beginning of the work. Make sure you are happy with paying a deposit, and never agree to make full payment before the work is completed satisfactorily.

9. Agree and sign a contract and schedule of works (see below).

Spotting the cowboys

There are some cowboys about, and you should take steps to avoid these people. Their work could be shoddy, incomplete, dangerous or far too expensive. Look out for the following signs, and if you are in any doubt you should find someone else to do the work for you:

■   Offers of cheaper work for a cash payment. These people are avoiding paying taxes, they are probably not insured and they will not be able to offer a warranty. You will have no form of redress if the work is poor, incomplete or defective. You will not be able to provide a warranty for a potential buyer to inspect.

■   A reluctance to provide references or details of previous jobs. The person is probably unable to do this because he or she does not have any previous satisfied customers.

■   A request for a large deposit before the work begins. Reputable builders will be able to source materials without needing an upfront deposit. Cowboys ask for a deposit and then disappear with the money or do not carry out the work to the required standard.

■   A reluctance to provide a written quotation. Cowboys will give a rough estimate and then charge much more than this figure when the work is finished, whatever the standard. They may try to convince you that a verbal estimate is a contract and that the work will be within this price range. Don't believe them. If they will not provide a specific, written quotation, move on to another builder.

■   A willingness to start immediately. Most reputable builders will be busy and cannot start the work so soon.

■ A reluctance to say when the job will be complete. Some cowboys will drag out a job unnecessarily and then try to charge you much more because they have been on site for so long.

■ A request to be paid per hour or per day. Again, the job will take much longer than expected.

■ A reluctance to provide contact details, except for a mobile phone number. Avoid these people at all costs.

■ They are very happy to criticize the competition and point out the weaknesses of other builders.

Developing a contract and schedule of works

When employing builders you need to write down exactly what you require. This specification does not need to be technical but should detail the work you want to carry out. You should discuss this specification with your builder and check that you both clearly understand what is required. It is important to develop a good working relationship with your builder, and if you find that you cannot communicate well, misunderstand each other or disagree about what is required, you should consider employing someone else.

Once you have reached agreement on the type of work required and you find the quotation agreeable, you need to develop a contract. The National Federation of Builders insists that members use a straightforward, plain English contract when undertaking work for homeowners and occupiers. This helps to avoid confusion and any potential disputes. The Joint Contract Tribunal (JCT) has produced a minor works contract that sets down in writing what is expected of the builder and the commissioning owner. It is a robust legal document that avoids legal and technical jargon. More information about JCT contracts can be obtained from www.jctcontracts.com.

The Federation of Master Builders (FMB) is a trade organization representing small and medium-sized companies throughout the United Kingdom. Members are carefully vetted and have to adhere to a strict code of practice. On its website you can access a free downloadable Plain English Contract for small and large domestic building work. Your name and that of the builder will be entered into the contract, and you can use the service even if the builder is not a member. Alternatively the contracts are available to buy from the FMB (details below).

The contract should include the following information:

- name and contact details of you and the builder;

- the price, including VAT;

- the payment terms;

- working hours;

- insurance information and guarantees;

- defects liability period;

- how to resolve disputes;

- what will happen if extra work is required;

- what will happen if the project takes longer than expected;

- completion date.

Any contract to which you agree should be easy to understand, and all relevant parties must inspect the small print.

Understanding the sequence of trades

Larger projects may require a variety of builders, traders and service providers to work on site. For everyone to work effectively and efficiently you need to make sure that the work is carried out in the right sequence. This is known as the 'sequence of trades'. Although projects vary depending on the work required, in general you should adhere to the following sequence:

1. Excavations.
2. Foundations.
3. Walls/framing.
4. Roofing.

5. Windows.
6. First fix plumbing.
7. First fix electrics.
8. First fix carpentry.
9. Insulation and ventilation.
10. Plastering/boarding;
11. Second fix plumbing;
12. Second fix electrics;
13. Second fix carpentry;
14. Fixtures and fittings;
15. Decoration;
16. Garden works (unless you have to access the garden through the property, in which case the garden should be completed before you decorate).

Before you begin any internal work you must make sure that the property is protected from the weather. This will save internal work becoming damaged. Also, by organizing the trades in the correct sequence you will ensure that previous work is not damaged and does not need repeating as subsequent traders begin their work.

Through careful management of trades you will ensure that problems are minimized, the site will not be too crowded or cluttered, workers will not be tripping over each other and materials will not pile up. All good project managers will ensure that the work is carried out in the right sequence.

Supervising the work

It is important to have a reliable person to supervise the work and to be on site or available while the work is in progress. This might be a task you undertake yourself, or you might appoint a project manager or supervisor (see Chapter 16). Effective communication is crucial – not all workers on site will understand the detail of your project. You or your manager need to be available to answer questions and check that each part of the project is being carried out correctly. You must understand that employees will not be as enthusiastic or committed to the project as you are, and you will need to check that their work is to the standard you expect. It is easier to spot problems early on and get them rectified immediately rather than have them put right at a much later stage. If you are unhappy with something, tell the worker immediately. Be forceful, but not rude.

As supervisor, you have to make sure that work is carried out safely and that the site is kept safe and accessible at all times. You also need to make sure that disruption to neighbouring sites is kept to a minimum and that noisy work is only carried out during the daytime.

If builders, traders and service providers have done a good job, tell them so, especially if you are hoping to work with them on another project.

Summary

Successful property developers build up a pool of conscientious, skilled builders and traders whom they can rely on to complete work to the required standard. It can be difficult for first-time developers to find the right people, but by making careful choices from the outset problems can be minimized. Workers also need to be well supervised and the work ordered in the right sequence to ensure that the project is completed to the required standard and on time.

If your project is small scale you may be thinking about tackling the work yourself. Before you decide on this option you need to think about whether you have the required skills, motivation and time available. These issues are discussed in the next chapter.

Useful addresses

Federation of Master Builders
Gordon Fisher House
14–15 Great James Street
London WC1N 3DP
Tel: (020) 7242 7583
Fax: (020) 7404 0296
e-mail: use enquiry form on website
www.fmb.org.uk
The Federation of Master Builders (FMB) is a trade association representing small and medium-sized businesses in the United Kingdom. You can find a member by using the online directory and obtain contracts for domestic building work free from the website. Hard copies are available for purchase.

18 **Doing the work yourself**

Carrying out some or all of the work on your property yourself can save you a large amount of money. However, you have to be realistic about what you can and cannot do, in terms of your personal skills, motivation and the time you have available. Also, there are certain jobs that the law requires to be carried out by a fully qualified professional.

This chapter guides you through the process of carrying out the work yourself by helping you to evaluate your skills realistically, pointing out the importance of adhering to Building Regulations, raising awareness of health and safety issues, making sure that you do not break the law and offering advice about planning your project.

Evaluating your skills and motivation

Some people get carried away with enthusiasm, only to find that in reality the work is too time-consuming and/or beyond their capabilities. While most of us are capable of developing the necessary skills given the right amount of time, as a property developer you might find that time is not available to you. Most investors need to receive an income as soon as possible, especially if they have a mortgage on the property. While a property remains uninhabited, that income is not being maximized.

Before you buy your property think about your own skills and the time you have available to complete the work. If you are in any doubt, set aside extra money to employ someone to complete the jobs you are unable to do yourself. When evaluating your skills and motivation, consider the following points:

- What work of this nature have you carried out before? How successful was the work? How quickly was it completed?

- Was there anything about the work that was not successful? What could you have done differently?

- Do you need to update/improve your skills? What local training is available? How much would the training cost? Is it cost- and time-effective to attend a training course, or would it be easier and cheaper to employ someone with the necessary skills?

- What available time do you have? Is it adequate to carry out the work efficiently and effectively?

- What other demands do you have on your time? Are these demands likely to change in the foreseeable future?

- Do you have a partner, friends or relatives who are willing to help you with the work? Have you had a frank discussion with them? Are they as enthusiastic as you are, and do they have the necessary skills?

- Will the work affect existing family relationships? Is everyone in agreement about what you are doing?

If you are in any doubt about your ability to satisfactorily complete any part of the project yourself, call in a professional for advice. Find out whether there is a charge for this service. If you have developed a good working relationship with builders and/or tradespeople, and you intend to use their services on future projects, they should be willing to offer advice free of charge.

Working within Building Regulations

Unless you have a sound working knowledge of building construction it is advisable to seek advice before you begin any work yourself. You can employ an architect, structural engineer or building surveyor if it is a large project (see Chapter 17). However, for smaller projects you can seek advice from your local authority building control officer or from an approved building control inspector in advance.

It is important to note that, although it may appear that the Building Regulations do not apply to some of the work you wish to undertake, the final result could lead to contraventions of the regulations. Also, if the work you are proposing affects the adjacent property in any way, you should seek advice prior to commencement. For more information about Building Regulations, consult Chapter 13; and for more information about the Party Wall Act, consult Chapter 14.

Working within the law

If you decide to do the work yourself, you are subject to the same regulation and controls as professionals. Minimum standards are laid down by law in the interest of health and public safety. They are there to protect you, your family and your tenants from unsound work that could place you in danger. Contravention of these laws can lead to prosecution and the possible imposition of substantial fines.

Before you begin any of the work yourself, you must find out about these minimum standards. Some work in your property can only be carried out by an installer who is registered with the appropriate government-approved body:

- Electrical installations should be carried out by a professional electrician who is registered with the National Inspection Council for Electrical Installation Contracting (NICEIC) or the Electrical Contractors' Association (ECA).

- Work on the gas installation in your property should only be undertaken by a professional registered with the Council of Registered Gas Installers (CORGI).

- Work on oil-fired appliances should be carried out by an installer registered with the Oil Firing Technical Association (OFTEC).

▊   Work on solid fuel appliances should be carried out by an installer registered with the Heating Equipment Testing and Approvals Scheme (HETAS).

New rules for electrical installations

In January 2005 a new law was introduced that demands that most electrical work carried out in households is only carried out by a 'competent' person who is registered with a government-approved body.

The law states that anyone carrying out work on fixed electrical installations in households in England and Wales must do so to certain standards. 'Fixed electrical installations' refers to wiring and appliances that are fixed to the building, such as sockets, switches, fuse boxes and light fittings. As a householder, developer or landlord you are responsible for proving that all fixed electrical installations and alteration work have been carried out in the correct way.

In addition to this, under Part P of the Building Regulations, you will have to make sure that the relevant building control body has been notified of the proposed electrical installation work, unless the work is to be undertaken by a person or organization registered with a Part P self-certification scheme. Electrical work that will need notification includes:

▊   a complete new installation or rewire;

▊   installation of renewable sources of energy, such as a photo-voltaic power supply;

▊   power or control wiring for a new central heating system;

▊   installation of a new final circuit, such as for a shower, cooker or lighting.

Electrical work that should not require notification includes:

▊   replacing damaged cables for a single circuit on a like-for-like basis;

▊   replacing an accessory such as a socket-outlet, control switch or ceiling rose;

▌ fitting or replacing an item of equipment that is currently used, such as a cooker, to an existing suitable circuit.

Rules and regulations are complex and you should seek appropriate advice from experienced electricians and your local authority before work begins.

Raising awareness of health and safety

Always be aware of the health hazards attached to any work you intend to carry out yourself. Conduct a risk assessment before you begin the work. This involves making judgements about the level of risk involved and deciding what you can do to reduce the risk to an acceptable level. If this is your first project you may find it useful to seek the advice and guidance of a fully qualified professional. The following steps will help you to conduct a risk assessment.

1. Think about the work you intend to do yourself. What are the hazards?
2. Decide who could be in danger and think about the way in which these people might be in danger. Think about the level of danger involved.
3. What can you do to limit this danger? What safety precautions can you ensure are in place? Write a list of all the actions you will need to take to reduce the risk. This will include a list of personal protection equipment you require.
4. Review and revise your assessment as the work progresses and changes.

A hazard means anything that can cause harm. The following list highlights some of the hazards you might encounter when your project gets under way:

▌ electricity;

▌ gas;

▌ ladders/scaffolding;

▌ chemicals;

■ asbestos;

■ falling debris/masonry;

■ rubbish/debris and its disposal;

■ confined spaces;

■ carbon monoxide, fumes and ventilation;

■ awkward/heavy weights and lifting;

■ black dust that can build up in gas pipes and valves;

■ lead poisoning from old lead pipes which must be replaced;

■ Legionnaires' disease (found in all types of large and small water systems);

■ Weil's disease (carried by rats and other infected animals, found in water and pipes);

■ faulty equipment;

■ fire (around 9,300 fires a year are reported as having an electrical source);

■ noise.

More information about health and safety can be obtained from the Health and Safety Executive Information Line: (0845) 345 0055, or from its website: www.hse.gov.uk.

Planning your project

Careful planning is required if you intend to carry out the work yourself. First, you need to decide what work is actually required and obtain the necessary planning permission (see Chapter 12). Seek professional advice if in doubt.

Next you need to find out whether Building Regulations approval is required, and if so, make an application (see Chapter 13). To do this you will need to produce a site plan and show that your building work will comply with the regulations. At this stage you should look into energy efficiency and find out whether there are any grants available that encourage the efficient use of energy in your development. For example, Home Energy Efficiency Grants are available to help owner-occupiers, landlords and tenants to install energy efficient heating and insulation, and through the Low Carbon Building Programme individual house-holders can apply for grants to help with the installation of renewable sources of energy for their homes. For further information contact the Energy Saving Trust (details below). At this stage you also need to make sure that your insurance is adequate and covers you and the property for the work you expect to undertake (see Chapter 14).

While you are waiting for planning permission and Building Regulations approval, update your skills where necessary by enrolling on a local course, reading up on a topic or spending time working with experienced developers. This is a good time to conduct a risk assessment and think about what protective clothing is required for each of the different tasks, such as safety goggles, gloves and masks. Find out what dangers might be present, such as asbestos.

You should then go on to plan the work in detail, listing the materials and plant required and researching the best places to buy equipment (see Chapter 19). All deliveries will need to be planned in the right sequence. This also applies to your sequence of trades, even if you intend to carry out all the work yourself. It is essential that your property is watertight and free from moisture and damp penetration before you begin the installation of electrics, plumbing, fittings and fixtures (see Chapter 17).

When you plan your project make sure that you stay within your budget (see Chapter 15). Think about how often you will use tools and equipment before buying specific items. Hiring may be a cheaper option in some circumstances.

Summary

Doing the work yourself can reduce the cost of your project considerably. However, you have to evaluate your skills and motivation realistically before you begin work. It can be costly and time-consuming to put right work that has not been carried out properly. You must also make sure that work is carried out to required standards and within existing regulations. These have been established to protect you, your family and your tenants, especially in terms of health and safety.

Whether you decide to do the work yourself or bring in others to help, you need to make decisions about sourcing materials. Through careful research and planning you can reduce the costs and make sure that materials are available when you require them, which will help your project to run smoothly. These issues are discussed in the next chapter.

Useful addresses

National Inspection Council for Electrical Installation Contracting (NICEIC)
Warwick House, Houghton Hall Park
Houghton Regis
Dunstable
Beds LU5 5ZX
Tel: (0870) 013 0382
Fax: (01582) 539090
e-mail: enquiries@niceic.com
www.niceic.com
NICEIC is an independent, non-profit making, voluntary regulatory body covering the United Kingdom. You can access a list of approved contractors through its website.

Electrical Contractors' Association (ECA)
ESCA House, 34 Palace Court
London W2 4HY
Tel: (020) 7313 4800
Fax: (020) 7221 7344
e-mail: info@eca.co.uk
www.eca.co.uk
ECA represents electrical engineering and building services in the United Kingdom. Search for a member using the online directory.

Council for Registered Gas Installers (CORGI)
1 Elmwood, Chineham Park
Crockford Lane
Basingstoke
Hants RG24 8WG
Tel: 0800 915 0485
Fax: (0870) 401 2600
e-mail: enquiries@trustcorgi.com
www.trustcorgi.com
CORGI is the national watchdog for gas safety in the United Kingdom. Its remit is to investigate gas safety-related complaints from the public and provide members of the public with details of local registered installers.

Oil Firing Technical Association (OFTEC)
Foxwood House, Dobbs Lane
Kesgrave
Ipswich IP5 2QQ
Tel: (0845) 65 85 080
Fax: (0845) 65 85 181
e-mail: enquiries@oftec.org
www.oftec.co.uk
OFTEC promotes excellence in oil-fired heating and cooking. OFTEC-registered technicians are individually trained and have their skills assessed and reassessed every five years. Find a member by using the online directory.

Heating Equipment Testing and Approvals Scheme (HETAS)
Orchard Business Centre
Stoke Orchard
Cheltenham
Gloucestershire GL52 7RZ
Tel: (0845) 634 5626
e-mail: info@hetas.co.uk
www.hetas.co.uk
HETAS is the official body recognized by the government to approve solid-fuel heating appliances, fuels and services. This covers boilers, cookers, open fires, stoves and room heaters. Useful appliance safety advice is available on the website.

Useful websites

www.energysavingtrust.org.uk
The Energy Saving Trust is a non-profit organization funded by the government and private sector, which works with households, businesses and the public sector to encourage the more efficient use of energy. On the website you can find information about energy efficiency grants offered by the government, local authorities and energy suppliers.

Sourcing materials

An important part of successful property development is to be able to obtain the right materials for the right price at the right time. This is especially so if you have a variety of builders and traders on site who are waiting to complete their work. Delays in obtaining materials can be costly, time-consuming and frustrating. If you intend to develop your property business you need to find out which suppliers can be relied upon to deliver on time and at the right price.

New property developers can find sourcing materials a difficult part of the project, especially if they are new to the area in which the property is located. However, through careful research and planning you can build up a list of reliable suppliers and avoid problems caused by delay, faulty materials and/or high costs. This chapter offers advice on effectively sourcing materials.

Hiring plant and tools

Plant and tools can be expensive. Hire or rental is a good option for property developers who are not going to use the equipment too often and who do not have a safe and secure place to store equipment when it is not being used.

When choosing a hire or rental company find out whether it is a member of the Hire Association Europe, as member companies are required to maintain certain standards of service, quality and equipment safety (see below). Although every company is bound by law to adhere to strict regulations concerning occupational and customer health and safety, some companies are more conscientious than others.

Always check equipment before it is delivered or collected, check the small print on the contract and make sure the hire company has adequate insurance cover. Larger equipment should have been checked and serviced since it was last used, and should contain a label as confirmation. You may find it useful to take direction from someone experienced in this type of plant and tool hire if you are new to the procedure. Good hire companies will provide a representative to assess your needs and discuss your hire options. They should also explain how to use the equipment and provide an instruction manual.

Decide for how long the plant or tools are required. Smaller tools can be hired by the day, whereas larger plant will have a minimum hire period. Most companies work out their prices on a sliding scale, so you could find you get a better deal by hiring the equipment for a longer period of time. However, you will have to sort out safe and secure storage overnight. It is not cost-effective to have equipment remaining unused while it is on hire, so you need to work out the sequence in which equipment is required (see Chapter 17). Plan in advance so that hire equipment is available and can be delivered at the time it is required.

As a property developer, you will be able to apply for a trade card with most hire companies. Terms and conditions vary between companies, so shop around for the best deal in your area. Some companies will offer substantial discounts on the hire price, a 'no deposit' facility and payment upon return, a fast-track service to equipment and a membership rewards scheme.

Disputes over damage to equipment and non-return of deposit can occur. Always read the hire contract thoroughly and check for damage before you hire the equipment. Make sure that existing damage is noted before you sign the agreement. You do not have to pay for fair wear and tear of any equipment you hire. However, you have a duty to take reasonable care of the equipment. The company is able to repossess the equipment if you do not comply with the terms of the agreement, do something that you should not have done, or do not give the equipment back at the end of the agreed period.

Buying plant and tools

Buying equipment might be a better option for property developers who intend to remain in the business for a number of years and who have safe and secure storage. However, even if you do intend to stay in the business for a long time, you need to think about unforeseen circumstances, such as business failure, a crash in the property market or changes in your personal life. Work out initial costs and take into account what might happen in the future when thinking about buying expensive equipment (see Chapter 1).

If you decide that it is worth buying some tools and plant, again shop around for the best deals, including a detailed internet search. Find out what trade cards are available and the rewards they offer. Ask about manufacturers' guarantees, and don't compromise on quality. Always negotiate and bargain, especially when buying expensive equipment and buying in bulk. Once you have found a good local supplier, stay loyal. In most cases your loyalty will be rewarded with additional deals and bargains. A good relationship with your supplier will also help to ensure that equipment is supplied and delivered on time.

Second-hand equipment might be cheaper, but you must know what you are buying and you must make sure that all equipment complies with safety regulations. If you are in doubt or inexperienced, seek specialist advice before you buy second-hand tools or plant. All second-hand electrical equipment should be checked by a qualified electrician before purchase. Buying through a private seller should be avoided as they do not have to comply with the same regulations as other suppliers and you won't have the paperwork for your purchase.

Remember that if you pay by credit card you may be able to make a direct claim to your card holder if goods are faulty or described wrongly.

Obtaining safety equipment

If you are intending to carry out any building work yourself, or you intend to be on site while this work is being carried out by others, think about the type of safety equipment you need. (If you have employed a project manager, he or she will be responsible for making sure that adequate safety equipment is provided. This information should be included in your contract.) Hire shops will supply some safety equipment, but if you intend to carry out a lot of the work yourself you should buy good-quality, hard-wearing safety equipment. This may include the following items:

- helmets/head protection;

- goggles;

- knee-pads;

- face mask/respiratory protection;

- gloves;

- ear defenders/plugs;

- boots with safety toe caps;

- safety signs;

- demarcation barriers and safety fencing;

- body harness/fall arrest;

- high-visibility/reflective clothing;

- circuit protection, residual current devices and circuit breakers.

When buying safety equipment make sure that it is 'CE' marked, which signifies that it satisfies certain basic safety requirements and in some cases will have been tested and certified by an independent body. Only buy safety equipment from reputable companies and manufacturers.

All safety equipment should be well looked after and stored properly in a dry, clean cupboard, box or case. It should be kept clean and in good repair, and all manufacturers' maintenance schedules should be followed.

Sourcing building materials

When obtaining materials buy only what you need to avoid product and financial waste. This means that you have to plan carefully, and if you are inexperienced, seek advice from a professional builder. You should also consider existing materials within the property and reuse these where possible. This will save you money and is better environmentally. You may be able to obtain salvaged materials from reclamation yards, local refuse sites, skips, charity shops and auction houses (details below). Try to source materials locally to cut down on transport costs and reduce the environmental damage caused by transportation.

Buying timber

When buying timber make sure that it carries the logo of the Forest Stewardship Council (FSC) as this ensures that it has come from responsibly managed forests. If you decide to reuse old wood check for rot, especially dry rot, which smells of mushrooms and has white spreading tendrils. Check that it does not contain woodworm, which is characterized by small round holes that may be filled with sawdust if the activity is recent. Make sure timber has not warped and is as straight as possible.

Buying bricks, blocks and masonry

If you intend to work with masonry you will need to make decisions about the type of stone, brick, blocks, cement, concrete, mortar, coatings and accessories to be used, in addition to making sure that you have the right masonry tools, such as mixers, trowels, floats, edgers and groovers. It can be cheaper to buy tools in kits rather than individually, but again, make sure that you don't compromise on quality and only buy tools that you will use. Remember to buy goggles, dust masks and gloves and read all safety instructions, especially in terms of skin and eye contact and what to do in cases of accidental spillage.

Replacing windows

Since April 2002 all replacement glazing has come under Building Regulations Control, which means that you have to prove that your windows comply with the regulations concerning energy efficiency. You can do this by obtaining a certificate from an installer who is registered under the FENSA Registration Scheme, or by obtaining a certificate from your local authority stating that the installation has approval under Building Regulations. Listed properties and buildings in conservation areas may be exempt from these rules, but you will need to seek appropriate advice from your local authority to check that this is the case. The British Fenestration Rating Council (BFRC) provides information about choosing the most energy-efficient doors and windows (details below).

Buying energy-saving materials

When buying materials such as loft insulation, draughtproofing, cavity-wall insulation and glazing, think about buying those with the energy-saving recommended logo, as this ensures energy efficiency and will help you to save money on running costs. Having the logo does not necessarily mean that the material or product will be more expensive, but you should shop around for the best deal. Contact details of local retailers can be obtained from the Energy Saving Trust website (see Chapter 18). Some local councils offer grants to help with energy efficiency – contact your council for more information.

Sourcing white goods

When buying white goods such as fridges, freezers and washing machines, make sure they are A rated. This means that they are more energy efficient and in the case of washing machines they will use less water. This will keep energy and water usage and costs down. That is useful if you live with your tenants and share the bills. It can also be a useful way to advertise to prospective tenants if you are interested in letting your property to someone who is concerned about the environment (see Chapter 23).

If you intend to become a landlord it is advisable to buy new electrical goods to furnish your property. However, if you decide to buy second-hand electrical equipment, you must receive proof that it is safe, either from the dealer or by asking a qualified electrician to inspect it. Keep all paperwork relating to the purchase and to any repairs or testing of goods.

Summary

Obtaining the right materials and equipment at the right price and at the right time is an important part of successful property development. Hiring equipment is often the cheaper and wiser option for developers who have smaller projects, lower budgets and few storage facilities. Buying plant and tools may be a preferable option for larger-scale developers. When hiring or buying plant or tools you must obtain the required safety equipment.

If you are intending to let your property you may need to provide some white goods and electrical equipment. You will also need to provide equipment to 'dress' your property for sale. These issues are discussed in the next two chapters.

Useful addresses

Hire Association Europe (HAE)
2 Holland Road West
Waterlinks
Birmingham B6 4DW
Tel: (0121) 380 4600
Fax: (0121) 333 4109
e-mail: mail@hae.org.uk
www.hae.org.uk
HAE is the authoritative body for the hire and rental industry throughout Europe. Members can join the Safe-Hire scheme that encourages professionalism and high-quality safety procedures throughout the hire and rental business.

British Fenestration Rating Council Ltd
44–48 Borough High Street
London SE1 1XB
Tel: (020) 7403 9200
Fax: (0870) 042 4266
e-mail: info@bfrc.org
www.bfrc.org
The British Fenestration Rating Council (BFRC) has developed
and operates a UK national rating system for the thermal
performance of fenestration products. On the website you can
search for the best-performing windows in terms of energy efficiency and search for installers, manufacturers and suppliers of
energy-saving windows.

Useful websites

www.aecb.net
The Association for Environment Conscious Building (AECB) is a
network of individuals and companies with a common aim of
promoting sustainable building. On the website you can find
information about: improving the environmental performance of
your property; choosing eco-friendly products and avoiding
damaging chemicals; using timber; planning and developing eco-
friendly properties.

www.upmystreet.com
On this website you can enter the name of your town or city and
find out the location of the nearest builders' merchant, DIY shop,
hire centre, plumbers' merchant and tile stockist. You can also find
out about property prices, policing, crime and neighbourhood
profiles.

www.salvoweb.com
Salvo is a partnership that aims to support dealers who hold stocks
of architectural salvage, reclaimed building materials, demolition
salvage and recycled materials. Where possible it encourages fair
trade and eco-friendly activities. Contact details for d\
suppliers and craftspeople can be obtained from the website.

www.nfrc.co.uk
This is the website of the National Federation of Roofing Contractors.
You can find a contractor, materials and related services in your area
on this website.

Stage Six
Presentation

Presenting your property to let

Once you have completed the required building work, you need to make decisions about presenting your property. When letting your property consider your target market before you decide on the fixtures, fittings and decoration. To attract tenants you need to offer what they need, want and like. If you do not do this you will find it harder to let your property.

Successful presentation involves knowing your market, decorating and furnishing appropriately and 'selling' your property to suitable tenants. This chapter offers advice on presenting your property to let.

Knowing your market

You must know your market before you decide to let your property. This will help you to decorate, furnish and price your property to suit your target market. When doing this, consider social demographics. Nationally, the population is ageing and there are more people seeking divorces. This means there are more people living on their own who may be seeking rented property. Is this happening in the area in which your property is located, or are the demographics quite different? Is it an area dominated by younger couples or single students?

Also, you need to consider how the housing market and economy are changing. Some people have decided to gamble on selling their properties while the price is high and then rent until properties prices have fallen, so that they can buy again at a cheaper price. Although this is a very risky strategy, it does mean that there are more of these types of people seeking rented accommodation. They will require short-term, unfurnished rental accommodation. Also, there are many more first-time buyers who are still priced out of the housing market, who will continue to find it hard to buy property unless prices fall drastically. These types of people will tend to require longer-term, furnished rental accommodation.

Chapter 8 offers advice about analysing the local market. In addition to following this advice, find out more about what your target market actually wants in a property. Unless you believe yourself to be very similar to this market, don't presume that you know what people want, as it is easy to get it wrong. Speak to potential tenants and visit properties that attract this type of person.

If you are interested in attracting students, speak to the local university or college accommodation officer and find out what price students are willing to pay, what facilities they require and the standard of accommodation expected. Don't presume that student accommodation is similar to what you may have experienced, perhaps 20 years ago. Students, or more importantly their parents, can be very discerning customers and expect a high standard of accommodation.

Older people who may have experienced a bereavement or divorce will require very different accommodation. They will have their own furniture and they might be interested in staying in the property for a longer period of time, because it is more of an upheaval to move. They may not require furniture, but they will expect the property to be well presented and comfortable. Carpets may be preferable to laminated flooring. Warmth and economic living will be important, and ground-floor apartments or single-storey accommodation will have more appeal to those with mobility problems.

Some corporate lets will require a high standard of accommodation, decorated to modern tastes with good-quality fixtures and fittings. However, other businesses will be more interested in good-value, basic accommodation. You need to find out what local businesses expect, and cater to their needs and expectations.

Choosing to furnish

If you wish to advertise your property as 'unfurnished', you will need to provide basics such as carpets, curtains and light fittings. Or you may decide to let your property as 'part-furnished' and provide occasional furniture such as beds, a dining table and a three-piece suite. A property that you wish to advertise as 'fully furnished' will need to contain most of the items listed below:

■ Bedrooms: bed and mattress (need to comply with current fire and furnishing regulations), chest of drawers/storage, mirror, wardrobe, bedside table, bedside light, desk and chair (if letting to students).

■ Kitchen: cooker, fridge/freezer, microwave, cupboards, work surface, crockery and cutlery, glasses, mugs, saucepans, kettle, toaster, bottle opener, corkscrew, can opener, chopping board and knives.

■ Lounge: sofa and chairs, coffee table, shelves/storage, lamp.

■ Dining room – dining table and chairs, shelves/storage.

■ Bathroom: sink, toilet, bath, shower, towel rail, toilet-roll holder, toilet brush, mirror, shelves, shaver point.

■ Garden: table and chairs, lawnmower and garden tools, storage.

■ Equipment: vacuum cleaner, ironing board, iron, brush, dust-pan, dustbin.

In general, your property should not contain items of sentimental or real value, televisions, video or DVD players, towels or bedding, unless you intend to let your property to holiday makers on a weekly or fortnightly basis. When buying crockery, glasses and mugs, buy cheap items that are easily replaceable. Avoid matching sets or fashionable items that will go out of fashion and be hard to replace. Simple, white crockery is best.

There can be big differences in what is provided in both furnished and unfurnished property. You and your tenants both need to be clear about what is included and reach agreement on this before the contract is signed.

Gardening and landscaping

Many tenants do not want to spend time gardening. However, that is not to say they do not like an outdoor space to use in the summer. You need to produce an easily maintained outdoor area that can be used by your tenants. Patio areas laid over weed-resistant matting or membrane are ideal. A small number of flower-beds, with membranes to protect against the weeds, and planted with a few hardy annuals, are useful to create a garden feel without providing too much additional work. Outdoor, weatherproof garden furniture and a party/barbecue area can add to the appeal of a property.

Lawns should be avoided, unless you are sure that potential tenants will want a lawn and be willing to mow it when required. If this is the case, you need to think about supplying a lawnmower and adequate storage for garden tools and equipment.

In general, the best advice is to keep gardens simple and make sure they are well tended between each let.

Decoration, fixtures and fittings

Paint finishes are more popular and easier to maintain than wall-paper. Keep colours neutral, in white, cream and light pastel shades to present a clean, fresh look. Depending on your market, wood flooring can be popular and gives the illusion of space. It can be easier to clean than carpets, but may need replacing if damage occurs. Neutral vinyl flooring is the best for kitchens, as it is easier to clean and/or replace if it is damaged.

White bathroom fittings tend to be the most popular and don't go out of fashion. Neutral vinyl flooring for the bathroom is preferable, as it is easier to clean and won't be damaged by moisture.

Decisions about carpets and curtains have to be made. Some landlords believe that it is easier to provide cheap carpets and curtains to be replaced fairly frequently. Others believe that it is more cost-effective to choose better-quality carpets and curtains that will last longer and need replacing less frequently, assuming that they are not damaged by tenants. All carpets and curtains should be in neutral colours, and patterns tend to show less dirt and damage. Expensive roller, roman or venetian blinds should be avoided as they can easily be broken by heavy-handed tenants.

Setting the rent

Many factors determine the level of rent. By now you should have done your research and found out what price is being charged for similar properties in the area. You will have checked that your property is being presented to a similar standard. If it is presented to a higher standard you may be able to charge a little more, but if it is to a lesser standard your rent will need to be lower. Monitor local newspapers and speak to local letting agents to find out how much rent is being charged and how quickly properties are let in the vicinity.

Consider the size of the property, the number and size of bedrooms, the number and size of bathrooms and the facilities within the property. All these help to determine the level of rent you are able to charge. If you are finding it hard to set a level, contact a local letting agent and ask him or her to come and visit the property and offer advice.

If you find that your property is not being let as quickly as you had hoped, find out why. It might not necessarily be that you are charging too high a rent. Instead it might be that you have targeted the wrong market with your décor, furnishings and fittings. Alternatively you might be advertising in the wrong place (see Chapter 22).

When people come to view the property, take their contact details so that you can contact them at a later date if they decide not to rent from you. They will be able to help you to think about your property and how it is perceived. If they say that the rent is too high, you will need to think about reducing it or improving the standard of your property.

Increasing your property's appeal

Your property is more likely to appeal to tenants if you take notice of the following tips:

- It should be clean and thoroughly aired, with no unpleasant odours.

- The bathroom suite should be clean, with the toilet seat down, no dripping taps and no unpleasant odours. The shower curtain and bathroom rug/mat should be new, and should be replaced between each letting. Black mould in bathrooms can be extremely off-putting to potential tenants, so you may need to replace mastic and grout and thoroughly clean tiles and surrounds.

- All painting and woodwork jobs should be finished. Touch-up where necessary between each letting.

- Make sure natural daylight is maximized by not overdressing windows or cluttering windowsills. If the weather is overcast or you are showing tenants around in the evening, make sure all lights are on, including a welcoming outside light.

- Make sure the garden area is tidy and inviting.

- Although you are not providing bed linen, make beds up to look cosy and comfortable when you are showing your property.

- The property should be warm and inviting, but not stifling. During colder months heat the property before you show tenants around.

- Think about the aspects of the property that will appeal to your tenants and sell them accordingly. For example, older tenants may want warm, comfortable and economical living. Point out the energy-saving installations such as loft and cavity-wall insulation and a new condensing boiler. Highlight the savings that can be made on utility bills as a result of these installations.

▌ If you are letting to students, think what will appeal to their parents, as they increasingly make the decisions about where their offspring will live.

▌ Consider simple touches such as cushions, table lamps and rugs to add a homely feel at little extra cost.

Summary

Think about your target market as this will help you to make decisions about how to present your property in terms of furniture, decoration, fixtures and fittings. You should find out what appeals to your target market rather than make assumptions about what they want and need.

You will find it easier to let your property if you have aimed it at the right market. Careful research is essential. Plan your viewings and make sure that you present and 'sell' your property in a way that will appeal to potential tenants.

Another part of successful property letting is to be able to advertise and market your property effectively. These issues are discussed in Chapter 22. The next chapter looks at presenting your property for sale.

Presenting your property for sale

Once you have completed your renovation, refurbishment or conversion project, if you do not intend to let the property you must make decisions about how you are going to present it for sale. To do this successfully you need to know your market and present your property according to its tastes and requirements. You also need to know how to sell your property to potential buyers, and make sure that you choose to sell at the right time, especially given current market conditions (see Chapter 1).

Chapter 22 offers advice about advertising and marketing your property. This chapter offers advice about presenting your property in a way that will appeal to your target market. It includes decisions about the market, producing a home information pack, knowing how to sell your property and negotiating with potential buyers.

Deciding on your market

It is important to think about your intended market early in your development project as this will help you to make decisions about décor, fixtures, fittings, furnishings, landscaping, gardening and 'dressing' your property appropriately. You will find it easier to make a sale if your property is furnished, and if it is presented in a way that meets the expectations of your intended market.

The location and type of property will offer hints about the most suitable market. Families might prefer larger houses in quieter locations with good schools and a thriving, safe community. Single, young people might prefer smaller properties finished to a high standard with access to a thriving social scene. Older couples might require a property that is warm, comfortable and economical to run, with a well-established garden and friendly neighbours.

Experienced property developers know the type of buyer that would be attracted to their property and they know how to present the property accordingly. Speak to local estate agents, find out what properties are on the market, and arrange a viewing. Visit show homes on new developments and take note of how the property is presented to the target audience. This will help you to think about your market and presenting your property in the most appropriate way.

Producing a home information pack

Anyone selling a home in England or Wales needs to put together a home information pack for potential home buyers. These packs are required for most residential property sales of homes marketed for owner occupation. The packs should include the following information:

■ An index that lists what is in the pack.

■ A sale statement that summarizes the terms and conditions of the sale.

■ Evidence of title.

■ The results of standard searches, such as local authority enquiries and a drainage and water search.

■ An Energy Performance Certificate that has been prepared by a qualified home inspector and advises consumers on which energy measures might improve the efficiency of their home, from thicker loft insulation and draughtproofing, right through to the installation of solar panels.

■ Evidence of ownership – this will depend on the type. Commonhold properties will require a copy of the commonhold community statement; leasehold properties will require a copy of the lease, information on insurance and service charges.

■ A New Homes Warranty, if appropriate.

■ A Home Condition Report (at seller's discretion – this was dropped as a mandatory part of the pack after pressure groups lobbied the government, but the HCR may still become compulsory at a later date).

■ Planning consents (at seller's discretion).

■ Building control certificates (at seller's discretion).

■ Relevant warranties and guarantees (at seller's discretion).

■ Other searches (at seller's discretion).

Packs will remain valid whilst your home is continuously marketed for sale, usually for up to a period of six months. After this time, if your house has not been sold you may need to update some of the information, such as the local authority searches.

Up-to-date information about the home information pack can be obtained from the Department for Communities and Local Government and from the official government home information pack website (details below). To find out about organizations producing home information packs, contact the Association of Home Information Pack Providers (details below).

From December 1 2008 anyone selling a property in Scotland will have to commission a Home Report. This will provide information about the condition and value of the property before offers are made. More information about these reports can be obtained from www.homereportscotland.gov.uk.

Selling tips

There are many things you can do to increase the chances of selling your property, as the following list illustrates:

■ Make sure the property is thoroughly clean. A clean house gives the impression that is has been well cared for, is easy to look after and will provide a healthy, pleasant environment in which to live. Clean windows are especially important – most viewers are drawn to these.

- Make sure the property is free from unpleasant smells and odours. Don't try to mask these by baking cakes or making coffee – most people are wise to those tricks. Treat the cause of the problem, and don't have pets in a property you are hoping to sell. Carpets and upholstery should be new or professionally cleaned. Avoid strong-smelling air fresheners.

- Think about your market and its requirements before people come to view, and familiarize yourself with these. Point out features that should appeal to the viewers: airing cupboards and storage space for families; power showers and entertainment space for young couples; easy maintenance and outside space for older single people.

- Make sure all small jobs are finished. Don't have leaking taps, fill and touch up any chips or gaps in woodwork, replace any worn wallpaper and freshly paint walls and woodwork. Replace stained or mouldy grout and sealant in bathrooms and kitchens.

- First impressions are important. Walk towards your property in the same way as a potential buyer. Think about what he or she will see: the state of the garden, the front door, the windows, the drive, the gate, the path. Make sure everything is neat and tidy. Replace or remove anything that spoils this first impression.

- Remove clutter but make sure the property is furnished, as furnished houses sell better than empty properties.

- Organize the rooms. Show that each room has a specific purpose, and match these purposes to your target market.

- Restore and point out period features.

- Lighting is very important. Maximize natural daylight if possible: remove fussy window dressings and net curtains. In the evening or on darker days, use lamps and soft lighting to create a warm and homely feel.

- Make sure the temperature is right – cool in the summer, warm in the winter.

■ A well-stocked, tidy garden will appeal to most people, but younger couples or single people might prefer a minimal garden with simple outdoor space for parties and barbecues.

Negotiating with buyers

Estate agents will negotiate on your behalf if you wish. As most work on commission, they should try to get the best price for your house. However, most experienced developers find it preferable to carry out their own negotiations as this enables them to maintain control over the process.

Always show that you are willing to negotiate on the price. Potential buyers are much happier to think they have negotiated a bargain. When you set the price for your property, add in a negotiation margin so you can be seen to reduce the price for the right buyer without losing out financially. Think about the minimum amount you are willing to accept, and don't be persuaded to go below this price.

At this present time it is a buyer's market, and you may find that people are making very low offers and are willing to wait for prices to be reduced. If you have managed your budget carefully, you will know the price at which you need to sell to make a decent profit. However, you will have to work out monthly outgoings such as mortgage repayments, utility bills and council tax when deciding whether or not to accept a lower offer. If the housing market continues to slow down, it may be preferable to sell quickly and make a smaller profit. Careful monitoring of the market is essential if you find yourself in this position (see Chapters 1 and 6).

Choose a buyer who seems to be the best prospect. This might not necessarily be the person who is willing to offer the most. You are interested in the person who is most likely to see the purchase through to completion. This could be someone not involved in a chain, a cash buyer, a first-time buyer or someone with a prearranged mortgage. Keep personal likes and dislikes out of the decision.

Once you have accepted an offer on your property, make sure that you and the buyer know which fixtures and fittings are included in the sale. You will need to be very specific about this to avoid misunderstanding and arguments as the purchase progresses. Try to establish a likely completion date with which you are both happy.

Put all agreements in writing and give a copy to the buyer so that you both are clear about what has been agreed. This should help to avoid confusion and misunderstanding. It is advisable to try to build a good relationship with the buyer so that problems can be ironed out quickly, and it may mean he or she will be less likely to pull out of the deal. Don't be tempted to consider other offers once the buying process has begun.

Summary

Through careful research you will come to understand your potential market and know how to present your property to appeal to this market. Your property should be presented clean and tidy, free from odours and in good condition. Furnished properties are easier to sell than unfurnished homes. The furnishings should show a particular use for each room and be presented in a way that appeals to the target market.

Once you are clear about your customers you can go on to market and advertise your property. To do this successfully you need to develop a coherent and strategic approach. These issues are discussed in the next chapter.

Useful websites

www.communities.gov.uk
This is the website of the Department for Communities and Local Government. Up-to-date information about home information packs can be obtained here.

www.homeinformationpacks.gov.uk
This is the government website that describes the home information packs in detail for industry and members of the public. On this website you can find up-to-date information about the packs.

www.hipassociation.co.uk
The Association of Home Information Pack Providers (AHIPP) was founded in June 2005 to represent people and organizations involved in the production and preparation of home information packs. On the website you can obtain information about what the organization does, along with links to organizations providing home information pack services.

Marketing and advertising your property

Marketing is not just about making advertising decisions, it is a broad concept that includes market research, planning and development, communication of product and services, public relations, promotion and sales. All successful property developers have to put in place a coherent, workable marketing strategy. This will help you to understand your customers, whether tenants or potential buyers, and to reach, attract and retain them.

This chapter offers advice about developing a consistent and coherent approach to marketing. It covers the importance of understanding your market, and offers insight into advertising and promoting yourself and your property cheaply.

Developing your marketing strategy

Marketing is the art of appealing to people's wants and needs in such a way that they become interested in your product or service. To market your property successfully you need to research your customers, finding out what they want and need and making sure that this is provided. One of the reasons that houses do not sell or remain vacant is that they have been targeted at the wrong market.

You also need to research the competition, analysing their strengths and weaknesses, learning from their mistakes and finding out about selling prices and rent levels. Another reason that properties don't sell or remain empty is that they are priced too high. Setting the right price is part of your market strategy, and needs careful planning and research.

Markets, trends and fashion change. Your marketing strategy needs to take account of this and you need to make sure that you are able and willing to change with these fluctuations. When developing your strategy think about the present and future conditions. Is there anything that could change your potential market in the future and how could you respond quickly to these changes so that profits are not affected?

Once you have aimed your property at the right market, think about your sales strategy. Now that you know your target market, you know what will appeal. It is up to you to sell these benefits so that people are interested in your property. A competitive edge can be gained by considering the following strategies:

- Offer an excellent service. Follow up all enquiries efficiently, quickly and with courtesy. It is important to remain on good terms with potential customers and tenants, especially as word of mouth is such an important, free advertising tool.

- Try unique packaging: when advertising your property, try something a little different rather than copying the strategies of estate agents. Differentiate your property from those of your competitors.

- Think about interesting promotions. Perhaps you might consider offering an 'open house' or other strategies to encourage people to view the property.

- Emphasize the benefits of your property.

- Satisfy specific needs of your customers.

- Offer a competitive price and show your willingness to negotiate.

- Test and modify your product. If you are not achieving a sale or letting your property, invite people around for an 'open house' and find out why people are not interested. Be willing to modify your property or price accordingly.

- Develop a consistent and coherent promotion strategy.

Advertising your property can be expensive. You need to work out an effective strategy that does not cost a lot of money. Advertising on the internet can be an effective means, as can placing an advertisement in the property pages of the local newspaper and using local estate agents (see below). If you intend to develop your business in a specific location, word of mouth can be one of the most effective, free advertising tools.

When a potential customer contacts you, find out how he or she heard about your property, and keep records. Over a period of time this will show you the most cost-effective advertising strategy, and you can eliminate those that do not work so well. It is important to monitor and evaluate the effectiveness of your marketing strategy on a regular basis so that you can respond to problems and make changes as soon as they occur.

Using estate agents

Using an estate agent to sell your property can reduce the amount of time and effort you would put into advertising it. However, check all contracts carefully and make sure that the estate agent advertises your property effectively and makes every effort to achieve a sale.

When choosing an estate agency, make sure it is registered with the National Association of Estate Agents or the Ombudsman for Estate Agents (see Chapter 6). An estate agency must by law give you written confirmation of its instructions to act in the selling of your property on your behalf. The agency must also give you written details of its fees, expenses and business terms before you make an agreement with it.

Fees only become due if you enter into a contract with the estate agent. The contract may include the phrase 'with sole selling rights'. If this is the case you cannot use the services of another agent, and if you sell the property yourself you will still have to pay commission to the estate agent. Also, if you sell your property after the expiry period of your contract, but to someone who was introduced to you by the estate agent, you will have to pay commission.

Some contracts instead use the term 'sole agency'. The estate agent is entitled to commission if you sell your property to a buyer introduced to you by the agent within the period of your contract. You would also have to pay commission if you were to sell your property through another estate agent during this contract period. However, if you were to sell your property through your own efforts you would not have to pay commission because you are not an estate agent. To be an agent, a person must be appointed to represent the interest of one party against the interests of another to negotiate the sale on behalf of one party. If an agent has a conflict of interest, he or she must declare this to you.

It is not very common for estate agents to have sole selling rights, and you should avoid this type of contract because it is so restrictive. Sole agency is more common, but some estate agents may try to include an internet clause in this, effectively converting the contract to sole selling rights. You should read the small print carefully and if you find this type of clause, move on to another agent unless you are absolutely sure you only want to advertise your property through that one agent.

Some estate agents use the clause 'ready, willing and able to buy', enabling them to charge commission when they introduce someone to your property. This means that you have to pay commission even if your property is not sold. This type of clause should be avoided.

The most preferable term is 'multi agency' as this means that you can have several agents working for you but only have to pay commission to the one who secures a sale. However, the rate of commission is likely to be higher on this type of agreement. For advice about dealing with estate agents and knowing your rights, consult the Move It website from *Which?* (details below).

Making a complaint

If you believe that an estate agent has acted unethically or unlawfully you should approach them first to find out whether the problem can be resolved. If you cannot come to an agreement with the estate agent you can register your complaint with either the NAEA or OEA, if the estate agent is a member. If you choose to make a complaint to the NAEA the association will investigate your complaint and take action if required. A breach of the rules by a member can result in a caution, reprimand, fine, reclassification of membership, suspension or expulsion.

The OEA, on the other hand, is able to award financial compensation and if you choose to accept this award, you do so in full and final settlement of your dispute. Unlike the NAEA, the work of the Ombudsman is to compensate you for any disadvantage you may have suffered. It is not to punish the agent and the Ombudsman has no remit to impose fines or serve other types of punishment on estate agents. More information about making a complaint can be obtained from the NAEA or OEA (see Chapter 6).

Selling privately

If you intend to sell privately you will need to produce details of your property. This information should be clear, concise, well worded, persuasive, descriptive and effective. Obtain details of properties from a variety of estate agents and analyse the way in which they try to sell a property. Look at internet sites and find out how people advertise their property, noting the good and bad points about the different types of advert. Why are some adverts much more effective than others? Why are some more believable than others? Why do some attract your attention, whereas others do not?

Produce a short summary of your property that includes the initial information people want, such as location, size and type of house, number of rooms, garden and parking facilities. Then you will need to produce a longer description of the property: facilities in each room (sockets, telephone points), size of each room, number of windows and so on. Be honest and persuasive, avoiding clichés and estate agent jargon. Include information about the general state of the property, and highlight any interesting interior or exterior features. Do not provide misleading or wrong information – this is against the law.

It is important to produce a photograph of your property. Potential purchasers want to see a photograph of the house from the outside, and many make decisions about whether to obtain further details based on this photograph. Don't be tempted to omit a photograph of the outside of your property because you think it may not appeal to potential purchasers. Instead use a good-quality camera and make sure that your property and land are clean and tidy and presented from the best angle. Take several photographs on a clear, sunny day and choose the best one. If you have rooms or parts of your property that you believe to be good selling points, take additional photographs and include them with your property details.

Using the internet

An effective way to sell your property privately is to advertise on the internet. There are a variety of websites offering to sell your property. A well-designed and well-managed site should be listed on all major search engines and in a variety of directories. Some also pay for banner advertisements and link to a variety of related websites. This will ensure that the website receives as many visitors as possible, all of whom have the potential to view your property details.

When advertising through a property website, find out how much you need to pay, checking whether there is a one-off fee, commission and/or final charges when your property is sold. Also, find out for how long it will advertise your property – it is best to find a place that will advertise it until it is sold. It is also useful to find a website that will allow you to display a photograph of your property and edit your details when required. Some property websites offer you free digital camera hire so that you can take a photo of your property.

If you are intending to develop your property business and have a variety of properties to let or for sale, you will find it useful to create your own website. This can be done cheaply, and once it is up and running, costs can be kept low. If you decide to follow this route, consider reciprocal links to other property websites and make sure you are listed in all the major search engines. If you have done this effectively there is no need to pay for internet advertising.

Using an advertising board

If you decide to use a 'for sale' board to advertise your property, you must comply with the Town and Country Planning (Control of Advertisements) Regulations 1992. Advice can be sought from your local planning authority. In certain designated areas you will need to seek permission to erect a board, and in all areas the board will have to meet the following conditions:

- It must be kept clean and tidy.

- It must be kept in a safe condition.

- It must not hinder or obscure official road, railway, waterway or aircraft signs, or otherwise make the use of this type of transport hazardous in any way.

- It must be removed promptly when planning authorities require its removal.

If the board relates to a building in multiple occupancy you must make it clear to which property/unit the board refers.

Avoiding marketing mistakes

The success of your business depends on successful marketing. There are some common mistakes that people make when working out their marketing strategy, and you should make sure that you avoid these:

- An assumption that you know what your customers want without speaking to them.

- An assumption that you know what your competitors are offering without visiting their properties or speaking to them.

- An expectation that custom will come your way without you having to work very hard.

- A belief that setting a lower price than your competitors will have the customers flocking to your door.

- A reliance on too few customers or the same customers.

- A desire to grow too quickly, without gaining the necessary experience.

▌ A belief that paying for expensive advertising is the best way to reach customers.

▌ A failure to monitor marketing and advertising strategies, so that you don't know the most effective methods.

▌ A failure to recognize that the customer is always right.

▌ An over-eagerness to sell at all costs. This may manifest itself as desperation, an off-putting and misdirected hard sell, pushiness, arrogance or unprofessional conduct, none of which will attract potential customers.

▌ Too great an attachment to the product. You can't be objective and cannot understand why all potential customers don't view your property in the same positive light.

Summary

Your property business will be more successful if you develop a coherent and effective marketing strategy. This involves customer research, competitor research, meeting customer wants and needs, selling the benefits, effective advertising and well-organised promotional activities. It also involves careful monitoring and evaluation, along with a willingness to change if a strategy is not working.

Once you have developed a successful marketing strategy you will need to show potential tenants and buyers around your property. You will also need to make sure that your property is well cared for by your tenants. This involves making careful choices from the outset. These issues are covered in the following chapter.

Useful websites

www.which.net/moveit
This website provides information on using estate agents, from explaining the legal terms and estate agent responsibilities, to providing advice and guidance on selling your property. You can also find information about the latest campaign to improve the services offered by estate agents.

Stage Seven
Preservation

Choosing tenants

In the last chapter advice was given about marketing and advertising your property to potential tenants. But once people have shown an interest in your property, how do you choose the right tenant? You may have set ideas about the type of tenant you would like. However, there are laws about discrimination when you advertise and choose your tenants, and you should be aware of these before you let your property. Also, you need to check on the tenant's suitability and draw up an agreement to protect both you and the tenant.

This chapter provides advice about using letting agents, arranging viewings, asking questions, obtaining references and drawing up a tenancy agreement.

Using letting agents

Some property developers decide that it is less stressful and easier to hand over the letting of their property to a letting agent. This can be a convenient solution for people who live abroad or away from the property they wish to let. Letting agents can provide a number of services, such as finding and choosing tenants, collecting rent and managing the property.

If you are thinking of using a letting agent, make sure it is a member of the National Approved Letting Scheme, as members have to work to certain standards and provide a certain level of service (see below). Check that it has in place the necessary insurance to protect your money if the letting agent should experience financial difficulties, and find out whether it has suitable complaints procedures in place.

Letting agents will be able to carry out the following services:

▊ Visit your property and offer advice on the type of action that will be required before you can let it. This may include repairs, refurbishment and safety checks.

▊ Arrange for any necessary safety checks to be carried out.

▊ Offer advice on the level of rent you can expect for your property.

▊ Offer advice on your responsibilities and legal requirements as a landlord, and discuss your tenant's responsibilities.

▊ Give advice about suitable insurance for your property.

▊ Advertise your property.

▊ Choose tenants and carry out property viewings with them.

▊ Draw up an inventory/schedule of condition.

▊ Arrange for the filling in and completion of the tenancy agreement.

▊ Transfer utility bills into the tenant's name.

Before you employ a letting agent you should receive a written statement of its services and prices. Compare prices and services between two or three letting agents in your area, as these may vary considerably. You can search for a letting agent by using the online database of the Association of Residential Landlords (details below).

Arranging viewings

If you have been successful in your advertising (see Chapter 22) you will have found some potential tenants who wish to view your property. Arrange a mutually convenient time to visit the property and show the person (or people) around. Make sure that you have the following information easily to hand:

▊ A copy of the contract, which includes information about the amount of rent (see below).

▪ A copy of the inventory. You can refer to this when the tenant wishes to know what is included in a furnished property.

▪ A valid gas safety certificate and relevant electrical reports.

▪ Some landlords find it useful to provide testimonials from previous, satisfied tenants.

▪ Examples of previous gas, electric, water and council tax bills so that the prospective tenant will have an idea of the costs of living in the property.

▪ A property manual. This will contain information useful to tenants, such as the day rubbish is collected; how to work the central heating; the location of pubs, surgeries, dentists and schools; photocopies of relevant instruction manuals for washing machines, microwaves and so on; the location of meters and stopcocks.

Knowing what to ask

During the viewing you need to decide whether the tenant will be suitable for your property. Find out as much as you can about the person (or people). Why does he or she want to rent the property? Where did he or she previously live? Although your advertising will have specified certain requirements, you need to confirm that these are still relevant. You may want to check whether the prospective tenant has pets, is a non-smoker and is employed, if these issues are important to you. However, you should be sensitive about how you ask questions. Think about them in advance so that you are well prepared and do not cause offence.

Some people may not be completely honest, but if you observe carefully and ask some well thought out questions during the viewing you will get a clearer idea. With experience you will find that you develop a good sense of who would be suitable for your property and who you should avoid.

Obtaining references

Ask all potential tenants for references that you can follow up later. Don't rely on typed references that are difficult to follow up. It is useful to obtain the address of previous landlords, but this is not always possible. Always find out in what capacity the referee is providing the reference.

To save yourself time only follow up the references of the person to whom you wish to let your property. If there is anything that doesn't appear right about a reference, think carefully about whether there might be a more suitable tenant. If you are finding it difficult to let your property you may feel that you do not have the luxury of obtaining references and choosing the best tenant, but you should still be as careful as possible because it will avoid problems and disputes in the long term.

If you decide to use a letting agency, find out whether it carries out a credit search and make sure that all references are researched carefully.

Drawing up a tenancy agreement

A tenancy agreement is a contract between you and your tenant. Although it can be a verbal agreement in England and Wales, you should always produce a written contract which is signed by both parties and witnessed by a third party. This will protect you in cases of dispute. In most cases in Scotland you must produce a written agreement for your tenants.

You and your tenant have rights and responsibilities given by law, and your tenancy agreement must not conflict with the law or attempt to take away the rights of your tenant. A tenancy agreement consists of 'express terms' that have been agreed between you and the tenant, and 'implied terms' that include the rights given by law and arrangements established by custom and practice. To avoid confusion and possible dispute you should clearly state your responsibilities and those of your tenant in the contract (see Chapter 24).

Assured shorthold tenancy agreements

In most cases, if you are letting your property privately and are not a 'resident' landlord, the tenancy is automatically an assured shorthold tenancy. However, if you wish to have a different tenancy, you can agree this, in writing, with your tenant. An assured shorthold tenancy means that you:

▌ can get your property back after six months (subject to court orders);

▌ may be able to evict your tenant if he or she causes annoyance to local people (subject to court orders);

▌ can charge a market rent;

▌ can get your property back if your tenant owes more than two months' rent (subject to court orders).

Some types of tenancy cannot be an assured shorthold tenancy, and if your property falls into any of these categories, you should seek further advice:

▌ business tenancies;

▌ tenancies of agricultural land or holdings;

▌ college accommodation;

▌ holiday lets;

▌ where the landlord is a 'resident' landlord;

▌ tenancies that began before 15 January 1989;

▌ tenancies where no (or very low) rent is paid.

Assured shorthold tenancies give a tenant the legal right to live in the property for a period of time. The most common type is a fixed-term tenancy for a specified duration, such as six months. A contractual periodic tenancy, on the other hand, might roll from week to week or month to month. During the time of the tenancy your tenant has: the right to control your property, so he or she could stop other people (including you) from entering freely; the right to certain repairs (see below); the right to challenge rent increases; and the right to request information about the tenancy.

Completing a tenancy agreement

It is usual practice for you, as the landlord, to prepare two duplicate copies of the tenancy agreement ready for signing. The agreement needs to be clear and unambiguous. If a court is ever called upon to interpret the agreement, it might rule against you if the contract is ambiguous or unclear on any point.

If you are a new landlord it is best to obtain an existing agreement that you can use to avoid potential problems. Some solicitors and estate agents supply copies of agreements, though there may be a charge for this service. Some local authority housing advice departments may also be able to provide sample agreements. The Residential Landlords Association has produced a tenancy agreement which is free to members or available from its website for a one-off fee of £5.00 (details below). It has worked closely with the Plain English Campaign to ensure that the document is easy to understand and clearly defines the obligations and responsibilities between landlord and tenant. The agreement has been updated to include information related to the handling of deposits (see below).

In general, it is good practice to include the following in your agreement:

- your name, the name of your tenant and the address of the property;

- the date the tenancy is to begin;

- the duration of the tenancy. This can be any length of time, but if it is to exceed three years the agreement must be drawn up by deed and you should seek advice from a solicitor;

- an accurate description of the property, including an inventory which should be agreed and signed separately (see below). This should include information about responsibilities for damage and breakages;

- details of whether other people are allowed to use the property, and if so, which rooms they may use;

▋ the amount of rent payable, when and how often it should be paid, and when it can be increased;

▋ the amount of deposit to be paid and details about the deposit scheme to be used (see below);

▋ what is included in the rent, such as council tax and water and sewage charges;

▋ information about the services you will provide as landlord (these are extra to your legal responsibilities – see Repairs below);

▋ information about gaining access to the property and the amount of notice required (see Chapter 25);

▋ a detailed list of tenant's and landlord's responsibilities (see Chapter 24);

▋ issues on which a tenant needs to seek your permission before acting. These could include carrying out improvements, subletting, having pets or smoking in the property;

▋ the length of notice you, or your tenant, must give if either party requires the tenancy to end.

Repairs

As a landlord you have a legal responsibility to carry out certain repairs to the structure and exterior of the property and to make sure that gas, electricity and water supplies are in safe working order (see Chapter 25). This is a legal requirement and you cannot get out of these responsibilities by adding clauses to the contract. Any such clause would be unfair and not legally binding.

When you draw up a tenancy agreement make sure you include a clause that states that a tenant must let you know as soon as problems occur. That way you will be able to fix the problem before it escalates and causes more damage. When a tenant reports a problem, let him or her know when you will be able to sort it out. Always respond as soon as you can. Not only does this enable you to repair problems within your property, but it shows that you are a responsible landlord and encourages the tenant to report other problems when they arise.

Unfair terms

The Office of Fair Trading (OFT) receives more than 200 complaints each year about unfair terms in tenancy agreements. These include clauses about financial penalties, exclusions of the landlord's responsibility for repairs and unfair termination or eviction clauses. The OFT provides guidance on unfair contract terms in tenancy agreements, and you should become familiar with these before you draw up your contract. More information can be obtained from the OFT (details below).

Producing an inventory/schedule of condition

It is essential that you produce an inventory for your tenants. This should contain details of fixtures and fittings, and describe their condition and that of the property in general. The inventory should be amended and updated with each new tenant. You and the tenant should check the inventory carefully at the beginning and at the end of the tenancy.

Many disputes with tenants involve the condition of the property at the end of the tenancy. If you are a first-time landlord you may find it preferable to use an independent inventory agent. The agent will properly and accurately prepare the inventory, including details of the contents and a description of their condition. More information about inventory agents can be obtained from the Association of Independent Inventory Clerks (details below).

Repaying deposits

Normal wear and tear on the property is to be expected, and you should not unreasonably hold a deposit for this. Also, if equipment you provide for the tenant fails through normal wear and tear you will need to decide whether to repair or replace the item. Again, you cannot expect the tenant to pay for this. You should make these conditions clear on the contract.

The Housing Ombudsman Service (HOS) will deal with complaints and help to solve problems between tenants and registered landlords, especially concerning disputes over the deposit.

All social landlords in England have to be registered with the HOS, and private landlords can choose to register on a voluntary basis. For more information contact the HOS (details below).

The Tenancy Deposit Protection scheme

In April 2007 a new scheme was introduced to protect deposits and solve disputes between landlords and tenants. This scheme applies to any deposit taken after 6 April 2007 from tenants on assured shorthold tenancy agreements in England and Wales. It does not apply to Scotland and Northern Ireland.

If you take a deposit of any kind it must be lodged into one of the prescribed schemes. At this present time there are three schemes available:

1. The Deposit Protection Service (DPS) is a custodial protection scheme in which deposits are taken and placed into an account managed by the scheme. The service is funded by the interest earned from deposits held and is free to use for landlords and letting agents. However, this means that you will not earn any interest on your deposit. All transactions can be completed online and you (and your tenants if they have received a deposit ID number) can access the deposit details online at any time. For more information about the scheme and to register your details visit www.depositprotection.com.

2. Tenancy Deposit Solutions Ltd (TDSL) is a partnership between the National Landlords Association (NLA) and Hamilton Fraser Insurance. From April 2008 it has begun to trade as 'mydeposits'. This is an insurance-based scheme that enables you, as the landlord, to hold onto your deposit. However, you have to pay a one-off joining fee to open your account and an annual renewal fee to keep your account going. There is a discount on the fees for NLA members. For more information about the scheme and to find out about current prices, visit www.mydeposits.co.uk.

3. The Tenancy Deposit Scheme (TDS) is an insurance-backed deposit protection and dispute resolution scheme run by The Dispute Service. Again, you will be able to hold onto deposits but will have to pay a fee to use the service. There

are different fee levels for different types of landlord and for those who are a member of a trade association. For more information about the scheme and to find out about fee levels, visit www.thedisputeservice.co.uk.

When choosing a scheme, you should decide whether you need to hold onto the deposit yourself, perhaps because you wish to use it to make repairs to your property, or whether you are happy to pass the deposit onto a custodial scheme. You will also need to think about how much you might lose on interest and consider how much you might have to pay in fees. As fee reductions are available for members of landlords' associations, you also need to weigh up whether it is worth joining such a group.

There have been a few teething problems with some of the schemes, in particular with landlords being unable to contact the organizations by telephone or online. In certain cases your local landlords' association will help you to solve the problems by taking up the matter with the relevant deposit scheme.

For more information about the Tenancy Deposit Protection Scheme consult the Department for Communities and Local Government website: www.communities.gov.uk.

Summary

Choosing tenants can be a daunting task for first-time landlords. However, with careful preparation and planning you should be able to avoid some of the more common pitfalls. Obtaining a well-worded and comprehensive tenancy agreement which is signed by you and the tenant and witnessed by a third party is the best way to protect yourself against potential problems and disputes.

As a landlord you have certain legal duties and responsibilities. Some of these may be specified in your agreement, whereas others are 'implied'. Before you let your property you should become familiar with these requirements. These issues are covered in the following chapter.

Useful addresses

Office of Fair Trading
Fleetbank House
2–6 Salisbury Square
London EC4Y 8JX
Tel: (08457) 22 44 99
e-mail: enquiries@oft.gsi.gov.uk
www.oft.gov.uk
The OFT provides useful advice for anyone who needs to draw up a contract or sign a contract drawn up by another person.

National Approved Letting Scheme (NALS)
Tavistock House
5 Rodney Road
Cheltenham GL50 1HX
Tel: (01242) 581712
Fax: (01242) 232518
e-mail: info@nalscheme.co.uk
www.nalscheme.co.uk
NALS is an accreditation scheme for lettings and management agents. Members agree to meet defined standards of customer service and must have in place the necessary insurance to protect clients' money. Members are monitored and may be withdrawn from the scheme if they don't meet the required standards. Find a member in your area by using the online directory.

Residential Landlords Association Ltd
1 Roebuck Lane
Sale, Manchester M33 7SY
Tel: (0845) 666 5000
Fax: (0845) 665 1845
e-mail: info@rla.org.uk
www.rla.org.uk

The Residential Landlords Association provides a range of products, services and advice to its members. It arranges free telephone support, produces a members' magazine, arranges meetings and training, and provides free tenancy agreements. There is a fee to pay if you decide to join, but then you are able to access information useful to you as a landlord, such as an assured shorthold tenancy agreement.

The Association of Residential Letting Agents
Arbon House
6 Tournament Court
Warwick CV34 6LG
Tel: (01926) 496800
Fax: (01926) 417788
e-mail: info@arla.co.uk
www.arla.co.uk

The Association of Residential Letting Agents (ARLA) is the professional and regulatory body for letting agents. Membership can only be achieved by those who are able to demonstrate that they have a thorough knowledge of their profession and that they are able to conduct their business according to current best management practice. All members are governed by a code of practice which provides a framework for ethical and professional standards. You can find a letting agent in your area by using the online database.

Association of Independent Inventory Clerks (AIIC)
PO Box 1288
West End
Woking
Surrey GU24 9WE
Tel/Fax: (01276) 855388
e-mail: centraloffice@theaiic.co.uk
www.theaiic.co.uk

The AIIC was set up in 1996 to represent inventory clerks and provide information to tenants and landlords. Members must agree to abide by a code of practice. Find a clerk by using the online directory.

Housing Ombudsman Service
81 Aldwych
London WC2B 4HN
Tel: (020) 7421 3800
Fax: (020) 7831 1942
e-mail: info@housing-ombudsman.org.uk
www.housing-ombudsman.org.uk

If you decide to register with the Housing Ombudsman Service (HOS) you may be able to receive help in resolving housing disputes and complaints from tenants. Find details of registered landlords from their online directory.

24 Keeping tenants happy

Letting your property should run smoothly if you keep on good terms with your tenants and if they remain happy in your property. By law your property must meet certain standards before it can be let to tenants, but there are other things you can do to try to ensure that your tenants are happy.

This chapter offers advice about the standard of your property and what you should provide. It helps you to understand your obligations and your tenants' rights, and provides advice about solving disputes, going to court and evicting tenants.

Knowing your obligations

Before you let your property it must meet certain standards. These include the following:

■ It must be structurally sound.

■ It must be free from serious disrepair.

■ There must be satisfactory facilities for the cooking and preparation of food.

■ There must be a supply of hot and cold water and of 'wholesome' water.

■ It must be free from damp and other conditions prejudicial to the health of the occupants.

■ There should be adequate heating, lighting and ventilation.

▌ There should be fixed sanitary ware, including a bath and/or shower, washbasin and toilet for exclusive use of the occupants.

▌ There should be effective sanitary waste disposal and drainage systems.

▌ All furniture and soft furnishings must meet the appropriate fire safety standards (see below).

▌ All gas and electrical supplies and appliances must be safe and in good working order (see below).

As a landlord you have a legal responsibility to repair the structure and the exterior of the property. This includes maintaining and repairing drains, pipes, gutters, doors and windows. You have to make sure that the installations for the supply of gas, electricity and water are maintained in safe working order. The property must be kept at a standard and fitness suitable for habitation.

However, you are not responsible for repairs arising from damage caused by your tenant, and you do not have to repair anything that the tenant has a right to take away, such as electrical equipment the tenant has provided for the property. As the landlord you also do not have responsibility for rebuilding the property in the case of damage by fire, flood or other inevitable accident. To avoid confusion and dispute you should make these responsibilities clear in the tenancy agreement (see Chapter 23).

Furniture

You must ensure that furniture and furnishings supplied in your property meet the fire-resistant requirements in the Furniture and Furnishings (Fire) (Safety) Regulations 1988. There should be a symbol on the label to indicate that it meets these standards. This applies to both new and used furniture. The only exceptions are when the furniture was made before 1950 and if you are letting your property only on a temporary basis. You can obtain a free leaflet which explains these regulations in more detail: *A Guide to Furniture and Furnishings (Fire) (Safety) Regulations* from the Department for Business, Enterprise and Regulatory Reform

(BERR) by visiting its website (www.berr.gov.uk) or by phoning the Publications Order Line (0845) 015 0010.

Gas

As a landlord you have a duty to ensure that all gas appliances, pipework and flues are maintained in a safe condition, and all installation, safety and maintenance checks must be carried out by a CORGI-registered gas engineer. An annual safety check must be carried out on each appliance/flue. These must be carried out within one year of the start of the tenancy, unless the appliance has been installed for less than 12 months. If this is the case the appliance will need to be checked within 12 months of the installation date. You must keep a record of the safety check for two years.

Any equipment found to be defective or unsafe will be isolated or disconnected, and you must get the appliance repaired or replaced. Failure to maintain a gas appliance is dangerous to both you and the tenant and can lead to prosecution, which could result in an unlimited fine or even imprisonment. More information about gas safety can be obtained from CORGI (see Chapter 18).

Electrics

Before you let your property you should have an NICEIC-approved electrical contractor carry out an inspection (see Chapter 18). He or she will test all electrical appliances, make sure that wiring and fittings are safe, and check for fire and shock hazards. If the report highlights problems, you will need to get them sorted out before you let your property. If you do not do this, and a tenant is injured through faulty equipment or fittings in your property, he or she might be able to take legal action against you. It is recommended that a formal inspection is made on change of occupancy, and at least once every ten years, or every five years if you let to students.

If you provide any electrical appliances as part of the tenancy, you are required under the Electrical Equipment (Safety) Regulations 1994 to ensure that the appliances are safe when first supplied. It is advisable to have an annual Portable Appliance Test carried out on all electrical equipment. Regulations may vary between local authorities, so you should obtain information specific to the area in which your property is located. Some colleges, universities and/or local authorities require extra tests to be undertaken if you are letting your property to students.

The cost of portable appliance testing varies, depending on the electrician that you use and the number of appliances that need testing, but should be in the range of £50–£70 for up to ten appliances. You can find an approved contractor to inspect your appliances from the National Association of Professional Inspectors and Testers (NAPIT) (details below).

Knowing your tenants' responsibilities

Your tenant is responsible for paying the rent on time as set out in the tenancy agreement. He or she is also responsible for paying utility bills on time. This might include gas, electricity and water bills, unless you have agreed to pay these bills, in which case the rent you charge will reflect this extra cost. The tenant will also be responsible for paying the council tax (unless all your tenants are full-time students) and the telephone bill if there is a fixed-line telephone in the property. If there is a television in the property it is the tenant's responsibility to purchase a TV licence.

Once in your property tenants have to act in a 'tenant-like manner', which means they must take reasonable care to ensure that they and their guests do not cause damage to the property or fixtures and fittings. They must report disrepair promptly and carry out minor day-to-day activities to ensure that the property is kept in a habitable condition. This includes changing light bulbs, keeping the property warm and aired, and avoiding pipes freezing and problems with condensation. They must also make sure that the property is left safe and secure when they are absent, and deal with their rubbish in the appropriate manner.

Tenants are required to look after the internal decoration, fixtures and fittings, but this does not include normal wear and tear. If your tenants damage or break anything they will have to replace it, but you should use your judgement on this matter.

Withholding a tenant's deposit because he or she has broken a glass or a plate is not a good way to run your business.

Tenants are responsible for maintaining all gas and electrical appliances that they have a right to take with them when they leave the property. To avoid confusion and dispute you should make sure that the tenant's responsibilities are listed in the tenancy agreement (see Chapter 23).

Understanding your tenants' rights

Your tenant has the right to live in the property undisturbed for the period of time stated in the tenancy agreement. As a landlord you do not have the right to enter your property without written permission, or interfere with the rights of your tenant (see Chapter 25). If you do, this could be seen as harassment and you could be prosecuted.

While your tenants are living in the property it is their home and they have the right to control over it. You must respect this and agree to conduct the repairs for which you are responsible when requested. When conducting repairs you do not have the right to enter other parts of their home (see Chapter 25).

Although they have the right to control over their home, tenants must seek your permission before they do any of the following:

▌ make improvements to the property;

▌ sublet or take in a lodger;

▌ run a business from the property;

▌ pass on the tenancy to someone else.

You should include these points in your tenancy agreement so that tenants know what they can and cannot do in the property.

By law you must provide your tenant with your name and address within 21 days of a formal written request from him or her. If you only have one or two tenants you might be happy to provide your address with the tenancy agreement. However, if you have many tenants who can and will disturb you 24 hours a day, 7 days a week, you might prefer to wait until this request is made before you provide your home address. All tenants will need to be supplied with a telephone number on which they can contact you or your agent in an emergency.

Solving disputes

When problems arise you should act quickly. Talk to your tenant, find out what the problem is and come up with a solution with which everyone is happy. Always make a written, dated note of the problem and the agreed solution. If any further problems occur, you can refer back to this written record.

If problems persist you may need to bring in a third person to help resolve the dispute. This person should be as impartial as possible. Often it helps both you and the tenant if there is a fresh, impartial voice to help solve the problem.

In some cases you may not be able to solve the problem through friendly discussion. In these cases you will need to think about obtaining further advice. You need to be sure of your rights if you intend to take the case further. In the first instance you can obtain impartial, confidential and free advice from your local Citizens Advice Bureaux or from your landlords' association, if you are a member. If you are still unable to resolve the problem and you wish to continue with the case, you will need to think about employing a solicitor. This can be an expensive option and should only be used as a last resort. If you decide to take your tenant to court, you don't need to employ a solicitor, but you should make sure that you find out as much as you can about your rights, and those of your tenant, before you start proceedings.

Going to court

If you are unable to resolve the problems you are experiencing, you may have to consider going to court. You can use a county court to help you to recover your land or property, and to obtain money for rent arrears and damage to your property. If you decide to take this course of action, seek advice from a solicitor or advice agency before you begin proceedings. Court staff can help you to fill in forms but cannot offer legal advice.

The court proceedings must take place in a court that covers the area in which your property is located. You can find the location and contact details of courts from Her Majesty's Courts Service (HMCS) (details below).

Courts deal with different kinds of possession cases and you will need to make sure that you choose the procedure most suitable for your case. Again, seek advice on this matter. The three main procedures are:

- Rented residential premises: this is the standard procedure for repossession of property and for claiming rent arrears. You will need to complete the relevant forms and present them to the court office. Guidance notes for completing the forms are available on the HMCS website, or advice can be obtained from court staff. A date will be set for your hearing and you will need to attend.

- Accelerated possession procedure: this is a quicker method of gaining possession which may not require a court hearing. However, you can only use this method if you have an assured shorthold tenancy and you are claiming for possession and the cost of making an application. You cannot claim rent arrears through this procedure. You will need to complete the relevant form and provide all the required written evidence, such as the tenancy agreement and the notices sent to the occupier. The court normally makes a decision based on the written evidence you and the tenant provide.

- Squatters: if you have a problem with squatters you can apply for an 'interim possession order'. This means that, if the order is successful, anyone occupying your property without consent must leave within 24 hours of a copy of the notice being served on them. If they do not leave within this 24-hour period they are committing a criminal offence and you can call the police. However, an interim possession order is not a final order giving you possession of your property, so you must apply for possession at the same time. A final order for possession will usually be made at a hearing shortly after the interim order has been made.

At a court hearing it is possible for a judge to do one of the following:

■ Make an outright possession order. In this case the tenant will be given a certain amount of time (usually 14 days) to leave your property, unless there are exceptionally difficult circumstances such as the tenant being ill. In these cases the judge may delay the order for up to six weeks.

■ Make a suspended possession order. The judge may decide that you have a good reason to evict your tenant but that it is not fair to do so. In this case the tenant may stay in your property subject to certain conditions, such as paying all arrears. If your tenant breaks these conditions you are entitled to ask him or her to leave.

■ Adjourn the case. This may happen if there is disagreement about the type of tenancy or if there is a lack of evidence. You may be given a new date for a hearing or you may be told to reapply when circumstances change.

■ Dismiss the case. If you have not followed the correct procedure in bringing your case to court, or if the judge decides you have no right to apply for possession, the case will be dismissed.

■ Make a money judgment. This is an order that says that a tenant must pay his or her arrears, regardless of whether he or she is to be evicted.

Evicting tenants

Most tenants are entitled to stay in your property until a possession order takes effect. However, if they have not left by the date the court arranged, you are entitled to arrange for a bailiff to evict them. Bailiffs must not use unreasonable force or violence when removing tenants and their property, and only bailiffs acting for the county court can undertake this task. If you attempt to remove a tenant and/or their possessions you may be guilty of an illegal eviction, which is a serious offence for which you can be prosecuted and/or receive a hefty fine.

Summary

As a landlord you want to try to keep your tenants happy in your property. Happy tenants tend to respect a property and will alert you to potential problems so that you can act quickly. You should respect your tenants' rights and treat them fairly. To do this you need to become familiar with landlord and tenant legislation. Problems need to be resolved quickly, before they escalate. Only as a last resort should you think about going to court and evicting your tenants. If you decide to do this, you must follow the correct procedures.

If you remain on good terms with your tenants, they are more likely to be helpful when you need to access the property to carry out routine repairs and maintenance. However, there are rules and regulations relating to the maintenance of let properties, and you need to be aware of these before you let your property. These issues are discussed in the next chapter.

Useful addresses

Her Majesty's Courts Service
Customer Service Unit
5th Floor, Clive House
Petty France
London SW1H 9EX
Tel: (020) 7189 2000 or 0845 456 8770
Fax: (020) 7189 2732
e-mail: customerservicecshq@hmcourts-service.gsi.gov.uk
www.hmcourts-service.gov.uk
HMCS brings together the Magistrate's Courts Service and the Courts Service into one single organization. On the website you can obtain details of courts and where to find them, information on procedures and processes, and forms with guidance for completing them.

Useful websites

www.napit.org.uk
This is the website of the National Association of Professional
Inspectors and Testers. All NAPIT members carrying out domestic
work in the United Kingdom are part of the government
Trustmark scheme, which signifies that a business has insurance,
good health and safety practices and good customer care. Also, all
NAPIT members are backed by a full six-year guarantee for the
workmanship. You can find a member by using the online
database.

Maintaining your property

In the last chapter advice was offered about how to establish a good relationship with your tenant. If you are on good terms with your tenant, you can trust each other to keep the property well maintained. This is important for your investment, as poor standards and disrepair are expensive to rectify.

You have a legal obligation to maintain your property and keep it at a suitable standard for habitation. To do this you will need to conduct repairs when requested, inspect your property from time to time, negotiate reasonable access and clean the property thoroughly between tenants. This chapter offers advice on these aspects of property maintenance.

Using property management companies

Some landlords find it more convenient to use the services of a property management company to manage their rental property. You may find this more convenient if you live a long way from your property or if you do not have the time or inclination to manage the property yourself. Property management companies offer advice on what needs to be done to your property to make it suitable for the rental market. They will collect the rent each month and provide you with a statement of account, visiting the property at agreed intervals to check that it is being well maintained.

Property management companies will also arrange to have routine maintenance work carried out, after agreeing expenditure with you, and respond to the tenant's enquiries, problems and emergencies. Prices vary considerably, so shop around for the best deal. Make sure you receive a written statement of services and costs before you employ someone to look after your property.

If you decide to use a property management company, find out whether it is a member of the National Approved Letting Scheme (NALS), as members have to adhere to certain standards of customer service and care (see Chapter 23).

Conducting repairs

As the landlord you are responsible for carrying out repairs to the structure and exterior of the property. Even though you may not need to gain access to your property to conduct these repairs, you should inform the tenant when you intend to carry them out (see below). You are also responsible for the heating system and all gas and electrical appliances, but you can only carry out repairs to these appliances if you are fully qualified and registered with the appropriate government-approved body (see Chapter 18).

If the internal decoration is spoiled when you are conducting your repairs, you are required to put right that damage. Also, you should note that if work is carried out unsatisfactorily or is left unfinished or in a dangerous condition, this can be construed as harassment and/or breach of contract and you could be liable to prosecution.

When your tenant informs you that some repairs are needed, you must act on this information. You will need to find out whether the work is necessary, and if so carry it out, or arrange for someone else to do so. If you fail to act on the information supplied by your tenant and do not carry out the required work, your tenant can sue you in court. The court can award damages and order repairs to be done. If you have been told about the need for repairs, and you fail to do them, local authorities have powers that require you to do the work. If you still fail to comply, the local authority can carry out the repairs itself and charge you for the work.

If your local authority becomes involved, it could serve a 'repair notice'. This requires that you make your property fit for human habitation and correct any disrepair that interferes with the personal comfort of your tenant. The local authority might also serve an 'improvement notice'. This requires that you improve your property to a certain standard and install certain amenities. However, if you are serious about investing in property you should not let any of your properties get into a state where this might happen, as you will lose money on your investment. This is of particular importance when property prices are falling and in cases where you may be required to make a quick sale, once the tenancy has finished. Also, in extreme cases the local authority can order your property to be closed or demolished.

Negotiating access

The law states that you must provide your tenant with at least 24-hours prior notice in writing if you want to access the property, or send in builders or other workers. This might be to check on the condition of the property or to carry out repairs or maintenance. This law does not apply in cases of emergency, and if your tenant is in agreement you may access the property without this prior notice. All access must be carried out at a reasonable time of the day. To maintain harmony it is best to negotiate a 'reasonable' time with tenants.

Bear in mind that you only have the right to enter the parts of the property that need repair work. You cannot use this access to check on other parts of the house unless you have the permission of the tenant. Also, if you want to carry out improvements to the property, you will need to add this to the tenancy agreement or seek permission from the tenant. However, the tenant might not agree to these improvements for fear of you increasing the rent or attempting to sell the property.

After you have finished the repairs or maintenance, discuss the work with your tenant and check that he or she is happy that it has been carried out satisfactorily, especially when it has been carried out by other workers. This will help you to check that the work has been completed to the required standard, and should help to reduce the number of call-outs from your tenant.

Cleaning

When a tenancy has finished, or when a tenant has left, you need to clean your property ready for the next tenant. This may be a task you intend to carry out yourself, or you may find it more convenient to employ the services of a cleaning company. If you decide on the latter, obtain a quotation and statement of services from more than one company so that you can compare and contrast services and prices.

Another, cheaper solution is to employ a reliable person to clean your property for you. He or she will come to understand what to expect, and will not be daunted or put off by the state in which some properties can be left. You must also prepare yourself for this. Although tenants are expected to act in a 'tenant-like' manner, some will not respect your property and will leave it in a terrible state. If you know what to expect it will not come as too much of a shock, and you can spend your time cleaning your property ready for the next tenant.

Replacing household items and furniture

It is the tenant's responsibility to replace damaged and broken household items and furniture. The tenancy agreement should clearly state the tenant's responsibilities in terms of replacing these items, so that major loss and damage can be put right by the tenant. However, for smaller items you will need to use your judgement for each case. Crockery and glasses are easily broken. If you have taken the advice offered in Chapter 20, you will be able to replace small items easily, quickly and cheaply ready for the next tenant.

The tenant is not responsible for any damage caused by normal wear and tear. Again, you will need to use your judgement about what needs to be replaced ready for the next tenant. This will depend on the type of property you are letting, the amount of rent you intend to charge and the type of tenant you are hoping to attract (see Chapter 20).

Between each tenancy you need to check furniture, fixtures and fittings to make sure that everything is safe and in a good state of repair. Replace anything that is broken or in such a poor state that it is not suitable to leave for the next tenant. There are some things that should be replaced for hygiene reasons and because it looks better for new tenants. This includes bath mats, shower curtains and some cleaning tools and equipment.

Remember that, if you intend to replace furniture and electrical equipment they must conform to the required safety standards (see Chapter 24).

Summary

If you have bought a property and are letting it for investment purposes, it is essential that you keep it well maintained and in good condition. This will help to attract tenants and the property will better hold its value, if and when you decide to sell. If you live a long way from your property, you might find it more convenient to employ the services of a property management company to carry out the repairs, maintenance and management. If you decide to maintain the property yourself, you need to be aware of the rules and regulations concerning access.

Becoming an investor in property is an exciting and challenging prospect, offering the potential for personal and financial growth. This is the case even in times of market uncertainty, if you make wise investment decisions. This book has guided you through the seven stages of property development: preparation, progression, procurement, permission, perspiration, presentation and preservation. Useful addresses and websites are provided at the end of the book for those of you who need to carry out further research. I hope you succeed in your development project and find it enjoyable and fulfilling.

Useful addresses

Government offices

Department for Communities and Local Government
Eland House
Bressenden Place
London SW1E 5DU
Tel: (020) 7944 4400
Fax: (020) 7944 4101
e-mail: use enquiry form on website
www.communities.gov.uk
The Department for Communities and Local Government (CLG)
was created on 5 May 2006 under the leadership of Ruth Kelly. You
can obtain information about HMOs, the new home information
pack and other useful housing information from its website.

Her Majesty's Courts Service
Customer Service Unit
5th Floor, Clive House
Petty France
London SW1H 9EX
Tel: (020) 7189 2000 or (0845) 456 8770
Fax: (020) 7189 2732
e-mail: customerservicecshq@hmcourts-service.gsi.gov.uk
www.hmcourts-service.gov.uk
Her Majesty's Courts Service administers the civil, family and
criminal courts in England and Wales. The service provides information for people who are thinking about initiating court
proceedings. On the website you can find contact details and the
location of your nearest court, and there is a separate section
covering housing.

Scottish Executive Housing Division
Area 1f, Victoria Quay
Edinburgh EH6 6QQ
Tel: (0845) 774 1741
Fax: (0131) 244 8240
e-mail: housing.information@scotland.gov.uk
www.scotland.gov.uk
The Scottish Executive is responsible for the issues of day-to-day concern to the people of Scotland, which include housing issues. Contact the Scottish Executive for information on the Scottish Secure Tenancy, housing benefit levels and the Rent Registration Service (Scotland).

Office of Fair Trading
Fleetbank House
2–6 Salisbury Square
London EC4Y 8JX
Tel: (08457) 22 44 99
e-mail: enquiries@oft.gsi.gov.uk
www.oft.gov.uk
The Office of Fair Trading provides useful information for drawing up a tenancy agreement, offering advice about how to avoid unfair clauses and terms in your contract. Publications are free and can be ordered or downloaded from the website.

Planning Inspectorate
Temple Quay House
2 The Square
Bristol BS1 6PN
Tel: (0117) 372 6372
Fax: (0117) 372 8443
e-mail: enquiries@planning-inspectorate.gsi.gov.uk
www.planning-inspectorate.gov.uk
The Planning Inspectorate processes planning and enforcement appeals and holds inquiries into local development plans in England and Wales.

Companies House
Crown Way
Maindy, Cardiff CF14 3UZ
Tel: (0870) 33 33 636
e-mail: enquiries@companies-house.gov.uk
www.companieshouse.gov.uk
The main functions of Companies House are to incorporate and dissolve limited companies, examine and store company information delivered under the Companies Act and make this information available to the public.

Building and construction

National Federation of Builders (NFB)
55 Tufton Street
London SW1P 3QL
Tel: (0870) 8989 091
Fax: (0870) 8989 096
e-mail: use enquiry form on website
www.builders.org.uk
The NFB is the construction industry's longest-established trade association. Members have to satisfy stringent entrance criteria, which include providing references from accountants, previous suppliers, architects and surveyors.

Federation of Master Builders (FMB)
Gordon Fisher House
14–15 Great James Street
London WC1N 3DP
Tel: (020) 7242 7583
Fax: (020) 7404 0296
e-mail: use enquiry form on website
www.fmb.org.uk
The FMB is a trade association representing small and medium-sized businesses in the United Kingdom. FMB builders work to a strict code of practice to which they must commit when they renew their membership annually. You can find a member by using the online directory.

Royal Institute of Chartered Surveyors (RICS)
RICS Contact Centre
Surveyor Court, Westwood Way
Coventry CV4 8JE
Tel: (0870) 333 1600
Fax: (020) 7334 3811
e-mail: contactrics@rics.org
www.rics.org
The RICS is the largest organization for professionals working in property, land and construction worldwide. RICS members have to adhere to a strict code of conduct and are required to update their skills and knowledge continually. All members have to have proper insurance and customers are protected by an RICS formal complaints service.

Royal Institute of British Architects (RIBA)
RIBA Client Services
66 Portland Place
London W1B 1AD
Tel: (020) 7580 5533
Fax: (020) 7255 1541
e-mail: info@inst.riba.org
www.riba.org
The RIBA is a member organization with over 30,000 members worldwide. It aims to 'advance architecture by demonstrating benefit to society and promoting excellence in the profession'. Only fully qualified architects can use the letters RIBA and title 'Chartered Architect'. You can find an architect by using one of the online directories.

Faculty of Party Wall Surveyors
19 Church Street
Godalming
Surrey GU7 1EL
Tel: (01424) 883300
Fax: (01424) 883300
e-mail: enq@fpws.org.uk
www.fpws.org.uk

Members of the Faculty of Party Wall Surveyors are experienced in the proper workings of the Party Wall Act 1996. They can be employed to serve the appropriate notices for you and see that the Act is properly implemented.

Chartered Institute of Architectural Technologists (CIAT)
397 City Road
London EC1V 1NH
Tel: (020) 7278 2206
Fax: (020) 7837 3194
e-mail: use online form
www.ciat.org.uk
The CIAT is internationally recognized as the qualifying body for Chartered Architectural Technologists and Architectural Technicians. Full members have to be fully qualified, complete an approved performance record and pass a professional interview.

Housing

National Association of Estate Agents
Arbon House
6 Tournament Court
Warwick CV34 6LG
Tel: (01926) 496800
Fax: (01926) 417788
e-mail: info@naea.co.uk
www.naea.co.uk
The National Association of Estate Agents is the largest professional estate agency organization in the United Kingdom. It represents almost 10,000 members and is committed to raising professional standards for those working within the property market. All members must operate to a professional code of practice and rules of conduct. A list of members is available on the website.

Ombudsman for Estate Agents
Beckett House
4 Bridge Street
Salisbury, Wilts SP1 2LX
Tel: (01722) 333306
Fax: (01722) 332296
e-mail: admin@oea.co.uk
www.oea.co.uk
The Ombudsman for Estate Agents has been established to provide a
free, fair and independent service to buyers and sellers of residential
property in the United Kingdom. You can find contact details of
members in your area from the website, access housing survey information and find out about their code of practice.

Chartered Institute of Housing
Octavia House
Westwood Way
Coventry CV4 8JP
Tel: (024) 7685 1700
Fax: (024) 7669 5110
e-mail: customer.services@cih.org
www.cih.org

CIH Scotland
6 Palmerston Place
Edinburgh EH12 5AA
Tel: (0131) 225 4544
Fax: (0131) 225 4566
e-mail: scotland@cih.org

CIH Cymru
4 Purbeck House
Lambourne Crescent
Cardiff Business Park
Llanishen, Cardiff CF14 5GL
Tel: (029) 2076 5760
Fax: (029) 2076 5761
e-mail: cymru@cih.org

CIH in Northern Ireland
Carnmoney House
Edgewater Office Park
Belfast BT3 9JQ
Tel: (028) 9077 8222
Fax: (028) 9077 8333
e-mail: ni@cih.org
The Chartered Institute of Housing is the professional organization for people working in housing. At present there are around 19,000 members in the United Kingdom and Asia–Pacific working in housing associations, local authorities and the private sector. The CIH is a registered charity and a non-profitmaking organization.

Leasehold Advisory Service
31 Worship Street
London EC2A 2DX
Tel: (020) 7374 5380
Fax: (020) 7374 5373
e-mail: info@lease-advice.org.uk
www.lease-advice.org.uk
The Leasehold Advisory Service provides free advice on the law affecting residential long-leasehold property and commonhold property.

Landlords and letting agents

The Association of Residential Letting Agents
Arbon House
6 Tournament Court
Warwick CV34 6LG
Tel: (01926) 496800
Fax: (01926) 417788
e-mail: info@arla.co.uk
www.arla.co.uk

The Association of Residential Letting Agents (ARLA) is the professional and regulatory body for letting agents. Membership can only be achieved by those who are able to demonstrate that they have a thorough knowledge of their profession and that they are able to conduct their business according to current best management practice. All members are governed by a code of practice which provides a framework for ethical and professional standards. You can find a letting agent in your area by using the online database.

National Landlords Association
22–26 Albert Embankment
London SE1 7TJ
Tel: (020) 7840 8900
Fax: (0871) 247 7535
e-mail: info@landlords.org.uk
www.landlords.org.uk
The National Landlords Association aims to protect and promote the interests of residential landlords throughout the United Kingdom. It has more than 100,000 members operating in the private sector. It provides a range of benefits and services to members including a telephone advice line, regular journals, meetings, events and fact sheets. You will need to pay a membership fee if you decide to join: details of fee levels are available on the website.

Residential Landlords Association Ltd
1 Roebuck Lane
Sale, Manchester M33 7SY
Tel: (0845) 666 5000
Fax: (0845) 665 1845
e-mail: info@rla.org.uk
www.rla.org.uk
The Residential Landlords Association provides a range of products, services and advice to its members. It arranges free telephone support, produces a members' magazine, arranges meetings and training, and provides free tenancy agreements. There is a fee to pay if you decide to join. More details are available on the website.

National Approved Letting Scheme (NALS)
Tavistock House
5 Rodney Road
Cheltenham GL50 1HX
Tel: (01242) 581712
Fax: (01242) 232518
e-mail: info@nalscheme.co.uk
www.nalscheme.co.uk
NALS is an accreditation scheme for lettings and management agents. Members agree to meet defined standards of customer service and must have in place the necessary insurance to protect clients' money. Members are monitored and may be withdrawn from the scheme if they don't meet the required standards.

Association of Independent Inventory Clerks (AIIC)
PO Box 1288
West End
Woking
Surrey GU24 9WE
Tel/Fax: (01276) 855388
e-mail: centraloffice@theaiic.co.uk
www.theaiic.co.uk
The AIIC was set up in 1996 to represent inventory clerks and provide information to tenants and landlords. Members must agree to abide by a code of practice. You can find a clerk by using the online directory.

Housing Ombudsman Service (HOS)
81 Aldwych
London WC2B 4HN
Tel: (020) 7421 3800
Fax: (020) 7831 1942
e-mail: info@housing-ombudsman.org.uk
www.housing-ombudsman.org.uk
If you decide to register with the HOS you may be able to receive help in resolving housing disputes and complaints from tenants. You can find details of registered landlords from the online directory.

Utilities

National Inspection Council for Electrical Installation Contracting
(NICEIC)
Warwick House
Houghton Hall Park
Houghton Regis
Dunstable, Beds LU5 5ZX
Tel: (0870) 013 0382
Fax: (01582) 539090
e-mail: enquiries@niceic.com
www.niceic.com
The NICEIC is an independent, non-profitmaking, voluntary
regulatory body covering the United Kingdom. The sole purpose
of the NICEIC is to protect consumers from unsafe and unsound
electrical work. It is not a trade association and does not represent
the interests of electrical contractors.

Electrical Contractors' Association (ECA)
ESCA House
34 Palace Court
London W2 4HY
Tel: (020) 7313 4800
Fax: (020) 7221 7344
e-mail: info@eca.co.uk
www.eca.co.uk
The ECA represents electrical engineering and building services in
the United Kingdom. It aims to promote quality and safety
through appropriate training and qualifications, and ensure that
all electrical and related installation work complies with relevant
standards. You can search for a member using the online directory.

Institute of Plumbing and Heating Engineering
64 Station Lane
Hornchurch, Essex RM12 6NB
Tel: (01708) 472791
Fax: (01708) 448987
e-mail: info@iphe.org.uk
www.iphe.org.uk

The Institute of Plumbing and Heating Engineering is the professional body for the UK plumbing and heating industry. There are around 12,000 members who have to be suitably qualified and adhere to a Code of Professional Standards. A Professional Standards Committee meets monthly to consider possible contravention of the code.

Council for Registered Gas Installers (CORGI)
1 Elmwood
Chineham Park
Crockford Lane
Basingstoke, Hants RG24 8WG
Tel: 0800 915 0485
Fax: (0870) 401 2600
e-mail: enquiries@trustcorgi.com
www.trustcorgi.com
CORGI is the national watchdog for gas safety in the United Kingdom. Its remit is to investigate gas safety related complaints from the public and provide members of the public with details of local registered installers.

Oil Firing Technical Association (OFTEC)
Foxwood House
Dobbs Lane
Kesgrave, Ipswich IP5 2QQ
Tel: (0845) 65 85 080
Fax: (0845) 65 85 181
e-mail: enquiries@oftec.org
www.oftec.co.uk
OFTEC promotes excellence in oil-fired heating and cooking. OFTEC-registered technicians are individually trained and have their skills assessed and reassessed every five years. You can find a member by using the online directory.

Heating Equipment Testing and Approvals Scheme (HETAS)
Orchard Business Centre,
Stoke Orchard
Cheltenham, Glos GL52 7RZ
Tel: (0845) 634 5626
e-mail: info@hetas.co.uk
www.hetas.co.uk
HETAS is the official body recognized by the government to approve solid-fuel heating appliances, fuels and services. This covers boilers, cookers, open fires, stoves and room heaters. Useful appliance safety advice is available on the website.

Finance

Association of Independent Financial Advisers (AIFA)
Austin Friars House, 2–6 Austin Friars
London EC2N 2HD
Tel: (020) 7628 1287
Fax: (020) 7628 1678
e-mail: info@aifa.net
www.aifa.net
The AIFA is a trade body representing all types of independent financial adviser. It provides information, advice and guidance to IFAs. As a member of the public you can use the online form to obtain details of IFAs in your area.

Institute of Chartered Accountants in England and Wales (ICAEW)
Chartered Accountants' Hall, PO Box 433
London EC2P 2BJ
Tel: (020) 7920 8100
Fax: (020) 7920 0547
e-mail: generalenquiries@icaew.com
www.icaew.com
ICAEW is the largest professional accounting body in Europe, with over 125,000 members. Members are required to adhere to their guide to professional ethics. You can find a chartered accountant by using the online directory.

Legal

The Law Society
113 Chancery Lane
London WC2A 1PL
Tel: (020) 7242 1222
Fax: (020) 7831 0344
e-mail: contact@lawsociety.org.uk
www.lawsociety.org.uk
The Law Society is the regulatory and representative body for solicitors in England and Wales. You can obtain information from the Law Society about choosing and using a solicitor and advice about dealing with common legal problems.

Ethics and social responsibility

Ethical Investment Research Service
80–84 Bondway
London SW8 1SF
Tel: (020) 7840 5700
Fax: (020) 7735 5323
e-mail: ethics@eiris.org
www.eiris.org
The Ethical Investment Research Service carries out independent research into corporate behaviour. This provides information for people who want to invest ethically, helping them to make informed and responsible investment decisions.

Housing Corporation
Maple House
149 Tottenham Court Road
London W1T 7BN
Tel: (0845) 230 7000
Fax: (020) 7393 2111
e-mail: use enquiry form on website
www.housingcorp.gov.uk
The Housing Corporation is the government agency that funds affordable homes and regulates housing associations in England.

HACT
50 Banner Street
London EC1Y 8ST
Tel: (020) 7247 7800
Fax: (020) 7247 2212
e-mail: hact@hact.org.uk
www.hact.org.uk
HACT is a registered charity and development agency that 'aims to develop and promote solutions for people on the margins of mainstream housing'. At present it has three main programmes: the refugee programme, the older people's programme and the supported living programme.

Shelter
88 Old Street
London EC1V 9HU
Tel: (0808) 800 4444
Fax: (0844) 515 2030
e-mail: info@shelter.org.uk
www.shelter.org.uk
Shelter is a housing charity that campaigns to end problems with homelessness and bad housing. Each year it helps thousands of people fight for their rights, improve their circumstances and find and keep a home. The charity will offer advice and guidance to anyone thinking about providing accommodation for vulnerable groups.

Empty Homes Agency
Downstream Building
1 London Bridge
London SE1 9BG
Tel: (020) 7022 1870
Fax: (020) 7681 3214
e-mail: info@emptyhomes.com
www.emptyhomes.com

The Empty Homes Agency is an independent campaigning charity that aims to highlight the waste of empty homes in England. It works with a number of organizations to provide solutions to the problem and bring empty property back into use.

Campaign to Protect Rural England
128 Southwark Street
London SE1 0SW
Tel: (020) 7981 2800
Fax: (020) 7981 2899
e-mail: info@cpre.org.uk
www.cpre.org.uk
The Campaign to Protect Rural England 'exists to promote the beauty, tranquillity and diversity of rural England by encouraging the sustainable use of land and other natural resources in town and country'. The website contains useful information about government housing policy and its impact on rural England.

Materials

Hire Association Europe (HAE)
2 Holland Road West
Waterlinks, Birmingham B6 4DW
Tel: (0121) 380 4600
Fax: (0121) 333 4109
e-mail: mail@hae.org.uk
www.hae.org.uk
The HAE was established in 1974 and is the authoritative body for the hire and rental industry throughout Europe. Members agree to comply with a code of conduct that covers issues such as standards of safety, quality, fair trade, service and insurance.

Useful websites

Government

www.statistics.gov.uk
National Statistics was launched in June 2000 and was set up to 'become the trusted source of the accurate and up-to-date knowledge we all need for the advancement of the government, business and people of the United Kingdom'. The site includes a wide variety of tables and reports on housing and property in the United Kingdom, including information from social surveys and the 2001 Census.

www.direct.gov.uk
This site addresses a wide variety of national and local government issues that are of interest to the general population. The housing section provides detailed information on buying, selling and moving house; private renting and letting; repairing and renovating your home; the planning system; and an A–Z of local councils.

www.neighbourhood.statistics.gov.uk
You can find statistics for local areas on a wide range of subjects which include population, crime, health and housing on this site. By entering the postcode of the property in which you are interested you can obtain summary statistics of the area based on the 2001 Census. A useful table shows you the average house prices of different types of property in your area, your county and in England and Wales.

www.communities.gov.uk
This is the website of the Department for Communities and Local Government. You can access information on housing policy, details of the national housing stock, and other useful housing information on this site.

www.hm-treasury.gov.uk
The Treasury is the United Kingdom's economics and finance ministry, responsible for formulating and implementing the government's financial and economic policy. You can obtain pre-budget reports and spending reviews on this site.

www.hse.gov.uk
The Health and Safety Executive offers information, advice and guidance on all aspects of health and safety. It offers advice on domestic gas, electrical safety and fire in the home. A range of leaflets can be downloaded from the website or ordered from the publication telephone line.

www.clsdirect.org.uk
Community Legal Advice is a service that has been set up to help people access information, advice and guidance on common legal problems. Through the website you can find a legal adviser or solicitor, download information leaflets and find out whether you qualify for legal aid using the online calculator. If you prefer to speak to someone there is a help and advice number you can ring: 0845 345 4 345.

www.fsa.gov.uk
The Financial Services Authority (FSA) is the independent regulator set up by the government to look after the financial services industry and protect customers. You can obtain information on financial planning, insurance, pensions, mortgages and warnings about scams, people and companies to avoid from this website.

www.voa.gov.uk
The Valuation Office Agency is an executive agency of HM Revenue & Customs. It is responsible for compiling and maintaining the business rating and council tax lists for England and Wales. On the website you can obtain information about who pays the council tax and find out the council tax band of a property in which you are interested.

www.landregisteronline.gov.uk
Land Register Online provides easy access to details of more than 20 million registered properties in England and Wales. You can download copies of title plans and registers in PDF format for £3 each, payable online by credit card.

www.ros.gov.uk
This is the website of the Registers of Scotland Executive Agency. It provides information about Scotland's land and property. On the website, for a small fee, you can find out about property prices anywhere in Scotland.

Banks and finance

www.hbosplc.com
This is the site from the merged Halifax and Bank of Scotland. The Halifax Price Index is available on this site and is a very useful tool for anyone interested in house prices.

www.oecd.org
The Organization for Economic Co-operation and Development conducts economic surveys, some of which are relevant to the property market. Abstracts can be viewed on this site.

www.bankofengland.co.uk
On this site you can access information about monetary policy, financial markets, financial stability and a variety of statistical reports.

www.aifa.net
The Association of Independent Financial Advisers is the trade association representing independent financial advisers (IFAs). Through this site you can search for an IFA close to your home.

www.icaew.co.uk
The Institute of Chartered Accountants in England and Wales is the professional accounting body of these two countries. Through this site you can find a chartered accountant, either by using the online directory of firms, or by contacting the relevant regional office or district society – contact details are supplied on the website.

Mortgages

www.cml.org.uk
The Council of Mortgage Lenders is the trade association for mortgage lenders in the United Kingdom. It is a major provider of market information, economic analyses and housing statistics. A useful mortgage calculator is available on this site.

Law and advice

www.lawsociety.org.uk
The Law Society is the professional body for solicitors in England and Wales. On this site you can obtain details about the Law Society, information about conveyancing, advice on choosing and using a solicitor and useful guides written for the layperson.

You can also search for law firms or solicitors by location or by name. The location search reveals the firms nearest your location first.

Building and construction

www.rics.org
You can find a chartered surveyor in your area on this website. The database holds details of firms offering surveying services and you can narrow your search to the type of surveyor you require.

www.nfrc.co.uk
This is the website of the National Federation of Roofing Contractors. You can find a roofing contractor, materials and related services in your area on this website.

Utilities

www.iphe.org.uk
The website of the Institute of Plumbing and Heating Engineering (IPHE) provides useful information and advice on various aspects of plumbing, with particular attention paid to health and safety issues. You can find an IPHE registered plumber in your area by entering the first part of your postcode.

www.niceic.org.uk
The National Inspection Council for Electrical Installation Contracting has been set up to protect consumers from unsafe and unsound electrical work. You can search for an approved electrical contractor in your area by company name, town or postcode. The website also contains useful tips for carrying out minor electrical work and important health and safety information.

Landlords and letting agents

www.rla.org.uk
The Residential Landlords Association provides information and support to UK landlords. The site has some useful information on tenancies, insurance and tax, but most of the information is only available to members. Non-members can access the forum, which might answer some of your questions on renting and letting.

www.landlords.org.uk
The National Landlords Association protects and promotes the interests of landlords operating in the private rented sector. Most of the information is only available to members, though there are some useful links and tips available on this site. You can also access its press releases – these provide up-to-date information on what is happening in the sector.

Ethics and social responsibility

www.aecb.net
The Association for Environment Conscious Building (AECB) is a network of individuals and companies with a common aim of promoting sustainable building through increasing awareness of the need to respect, protect, preserve and enhance the environment. On the website you can find information about: improving the environmental performance of your property; choosing eco-friendly products and avoiding damaging chemicals; using timber; planning and developing eco-friendly properties.

Materials

www.upmystreet.com
On this website you can enter the name of your town or city and find out the location of the nearest builder's merchant, DIY shop, hire centre, plumber's merchant and tile stockist.

Index

Index of advertisers